From Memory to Memorial

A KEYSTONE BOOK®

Keystone Books are intended to serve the
citizens of Pennsylvania. They are accessible,
well-researched explorations into the
history, culture, society, and environment
of the Keystone State as part of the Middle
Atlantic region.

FROM MEMORY TO
MEMORIAL

SHANKSVILLE, AMERICA,
AND FLIGHT 93

J. WILLIAM THOMPSON

THE PENNSYLVANIA STATE UNIVERSITY PRESS
UNIVERSITY PARK, PENNSYLVANIA

Library of Congress Cataloging-in-
Publication Data

Names: Thompson, J. William, author.
Title: From memory to memorial : Shanks-
    ville, America, and Flight 93 / J. William
    Thompson.
Description: University Park, Pennsylvania :
    The Pennsylvania State University Press,
    [2017] | "A Keystone book." | Includes
    bibliographical references and index.
Summary: "Explores the aftermath of 9/11
    in Shanksville, Pennsylvania. Describes
    how the local community remembered
    the event and how it was affected by
    national media attention. Follows the
    creation of the national memorial built
    at the site to honor those aboard Flight
    93"—Provided by publisher.
Identifiers: LCCN 2016021313 | ISBN
    9780271076997 (pbk. : alk. paper)
Subjects: LCSH: United Airlines Flight 93
    Hijacking Incident, 2001. | Flight 93
    National Memorial (Pa.)—History. |
    Shanksville (Pa.)—History.
Classification: LCC HV6432.7 .T558 2017 |
    DDC 974.8/79—dc23
LC record available at https://lccn.loc.
    gov/2016021313

Typeset by
Regina Starace

Printed and bound by
Sheridan Books

Composed in
Scala and Scala Sans

Printed on
Natures Natural

Contents

Prologue: A Journey in the Name of Memory

Lo que te importa en la vida no es lo que te ocurre, sino qué recuerdas y cómo lo recuerdas. (What matters in life is not what happens to you but what you remember and how you remember it.)
—GABRIEL GARCIA MARQUEZ

A very tall steel angel, in silhouette, pointed me toward the crash site. It was a beautifully sunny September day, and I'd driven up from Washington, D.C., via the old Lincoln Highway that runs across Pennsylvania. Productive farms alternated with lush woodlands and historic Pennsylvania towns until the highway took a steep upward turn and emerged on a high plateau. Now here I was, meandering down two-lane country roads, without the benefit of signage, trying to find the place where United Flight 93 had slammed into the earth five years earlier. It was a relief to see the angel mutely pointing the way.

I'd come here partly out of professional curiosity. As the editor of a national magazine about the design of parks and landscapes, I'd become deeply interested in, and more than a little concerned about, the way disaster memorials in public landscapes increasingly reflected the tide of mass killings in this country.

During my years at *Landscape Architecture*, memorials had been built on the site of the Oklahoma City bombing and at Columbine High School, and one was planned in response to the Virginia Tech shootings. As the crop of such memorials continued to grow, I had begun to wonder whether they fulfilled their stated purpose. Would traditional stone-and-mortar memorials really help keep memories alive or help heal those whose loved ones had been killed at random?

There was a more personal reason for this trip, however. My home is in Washington, D.C., and the editorial office where I worked every day lay three blocks east of the White House and six blocks west of the Capitol—the most likely targets for the fourth 9/11 airliner. That day, I'd been far too close for comfort to Flight 93's destination. That plane never reached its intended target, we were told, because the passengers and crew had revolted—the first such revolt in the history of airline hijackings—and had overpowered the terrorist hijackers, almost winning back control of the airliner before the terrorist pilot drove it into the ground at five hundred miles an hour.

Apparently, the bravery of the passengers and crew had kept me out of danger and saved me from witnessing the fire and mayhem that were visited on the Pentagon and the Twin Towers. Hence, this Pennsylvania countryside had a certain emotional resonance for me. So here I was, driving down the crooked road that led down and then back up to a makeshift temporary memorial set up by the local people: a tall chain-link fence adorned with flags and hundreds of other mementoes. A metal shed held a guestbook, scrapbooks of photos, and news clippings.

The crash site, which lay downhill at the bottom of a topographic bowl of land, was something of a letdown. It was a former strip mine, bare and featureless, and the actual point of impact had been backfilled so that there was literally nothing to see—and anyway, it was off-limits to visitors. I'm not sure what I expected, but I would have been content with a trail around the crash site where I could have hiked and pondered the meaning of it all. The temporary memorial—hemmed in by a guardrail and abuzz with visitors—was the exact opposite of that.

Still, most Americans who made pilgrimages here didn't need to ponder its meaning. They knew. There had been an attack on the nation, and there could be only one proper response: solidarity with the passengers and crew who took the fight back to the terrorists.

The attacks on the Twin Towers and the Pentagon had targeted urban centers. This one had a different resonance: deflected from the capital, it had struck the heartland. And these visitors' responses at the temporary memorial came straight from the heart. On the chain-link fence they hung caps, flags, license plates, fire department insignia, teddy bears, and various other trinkets on which they'd scrawled out their patriotism and prayers in black marker.

The only apparent requirement for the tributes was that they be material, tangible. And that was the whole point of the people's memorial—to be able to leave some physical signature, even if it was only a cheap consumer item from a big-box store on which you penned a heartfelt note. Placing something at the site indicated that

FIG. 1 The temporary memorial, erected by local people, at the Flight 93 crash site.
Photo: National Park Service.

someone remembered—and judging by inscriptions such as *Never Forget*, visitors felt they had a duty to remember what happened here.

The visual effect of all these mass-produced goods dangling from a chain-link fence took me aback. The homemade memorial bordered on tacky. But so what? This fence was a perfectly democratic expression of the thousands of Americans who had made pilgrimages here before me.

• • •

Whatever I or anyone else might have thought of the people's memorial, however, its days were numbered even when I first visited in 2006. Big plans were developing—although by fits and starts—for a permanent memorial at the crash site.

The National Park Service, guardian of the nation's historic sites, had been charged in late 2001 with creating a national park surrounding a proper memorial on this land. The Park Service had set up an office in Somerset, the county seat, and created an impressive volunteer organization to plan and raise money for a permanent national memorial.

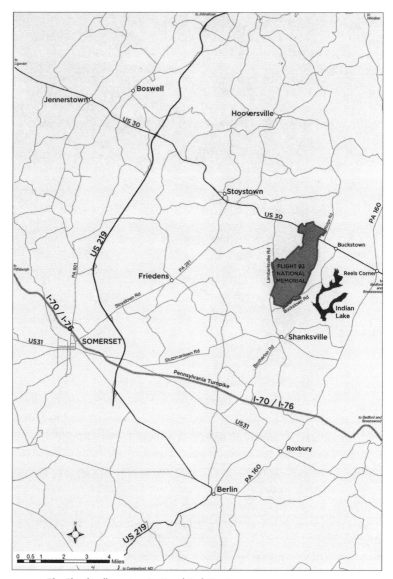

MAP 1   The Shanksville region. National Park Service.

The families of the victims had organized and were working with the Park Service, determined to enshrine the story of the passenger revolt for all time. The Park Service had already established the boundaries of the park—a sizeable piece of land that reached two miles from the crash site to the old Lincoln Highway.

The Park Service had also sponsored an international design competition that received more than a thousand entries. This was a "first" for the Park Service: a national park that was to be designed by competition. Some of the entrants had never designed anything in their lives before but were moved by what the passengers and crew of Flight 93 had done; others came from the ranks of professional artists, architects, and landscape architects.

A jury made up of design professionals, family members, and locals pored through the hundreds of entries before reducing them to a handful of finalists. From these they selected the winning design, "Crescent of Embrace," by an architect from Beverly Hills, California. Its presentation drawings showed a great semicircle of red maples around a low, sleek memorial wall at the point where Flight 93 came to ground.

· · ·

On the afternoon of my first visit, however, a permanent memorial for the Flight 93 site was by no means assured.

The winning memorial design had stirred up a blaze of controversy. In the presentation drawings, the crescent of red maples bore an eerie resemblance to the crescent symbol used on Islamic flags. A local preacher had spread a rumor that the Crescent of Embrace was an antipatriotic homage to the religion of the terrorists who perpetrated 9/11. Conspiracy theorists weighed in on Internet sites, claiming that Flight 93 never really crashed here—it was all a ruse by the federal government to deceive the American people. Others believed that the government itself had shot the plane down.

A far greater problem was that the Park Service didn't own all the land for the new national park. Much of the property was still in the hands of the coal companies who had strip-mined it, and they were in no hurry to sell it to the Park Service. As a result, five years after 9/11 not one shovelful of dirt had been turned, and it was unclear when any would be turned. By contrast, construction was already in full swing at the Pentagon 9/11 memorial outside Washington, D.C., where land ownership was never an issue.

All in all, the future of anything permanent on this site seemed very uncertain. Conflict swirled around a place that many Americans regarded as a shrine. The only thing that showed that something momentous had happened here was a homemade memorial, and the crash site seemed almost in a state of suspended animation.

Over the next several years, with ever more frequent visits to the crash site, which ultimately resulted in my writing these pages, three xiv overriding questions would emerge. All of them flowed out of that peculiar habit we have as humans of wanting to hold on to memories, which by nature are very transient and very frail. The questions were these.

What was it about this landscape and this place that had hindered the creation of any permanent memorial, ultimately stretching to a decade of delay? I was familiar, from my magazine work, with the usual processes of planning, funding, and building memorials, even ones created in the glare of national attention. What made this one unusually difficult?

If a permanent memorial were eventually built, *what built form would best express what happened in the skies above this place?* Were conventional styles of memorial—symbolic structures in marble, bronze, and granite, derived from Roman architecture and signifying social unity—really appropriate to a twenty-first century tragedy? Or were there new forms that would carry memory more effectively in a globalized and digital age?

Most important, and hardest to fathom, was a third question: *How does the memory of a terrible event shape or reshape the lives of people who live in its aftermath?* The people of the nearby village of Shanksville, Pennsylvania, would henceforth inhabit a town that was known for a mass murder. What effect would that fact have on their personal stories?

● ● ●

The temporary memorial included a semicircle of crude benches. A middle-aged blond woman positioned herself in front of them and began to speak to the handful of people assembled there. Her name was Sally, and she was one of the "ambassadors"—some forty-five local volunteers who greeted visitors to the site. I sat down on one of the benches to listen.

Sally lived just on the other side of the trees, she said. She had felt the impact of the Boeing 757 and smelled the jet fuel when it crashed.

She showed us a scrapbook of the forty passengers and crew. "They were the heroes," she said. "They all made a difference that day."

The ambassadors, said Sally, "are the caretakers of this place. We do this for the Flight 93 families. I believe you'd do the same."

Listening to Sally, it dawned on me that the temporary memorial wasn't meant for self-styled philosophers to be alone with their thoughts. It was a blunt, unapologetic celebration of patriotism and sacrifice. All that mattered here was that, in a time of great crisis, the country had pulled together. When Sally stopped talking, I had to wipe my eyes.

I wondered: When some sleek and serene design conceived by a professional architect replaced this scrappy, democratic memorial, would visitors still feel moved to tears? I'd reviewed many avant-garde designs in my work at the landscape magazine and had seen firsthand that they were not always the people's choice.

I recalled a stylish, award-winning New York City plaza designed by a famous landscape architect that was more or less deserted by the public, while a homely, old-fashioned park across the street, with shade trees and comfortable benches, drew big lunch-hour crowds. Would the sleek Flight 93 memorial draw as big and as devoted crowds as did this spontaneous memorial that the locals had built?

What is important in making a memorial, in what you remember, and in how you remember it? I sat a bit longer where I'd listened to Sally, then got up and walked to the parking lot. But I realized I'd forgotten something. I walked back to the temporary memorial's tin shed and wrote in the guest book, "Bill Thompson, downtown Washington, D.C.—the Target. Thank you."

I

THE DAY THE SKY
FELL DOWN

It was a beautiful morning to be working on the roof. Not a cloud in the sky. When Robyn Blanset drove up to the farmhouse, her father, Ray Stevens, was already up there with his tools out, finishing work around the chimney. Robyn got the stroller out of her car and put her little girl, Twila, in it. Normally, she would give Twila snacks to keep her occupied while she was on the roof, but this morning a black cat wandered out of nowhere.

The black cat was a stray who knew Twila, and it jumped in the stroller with her, giving Robyn an opening to climb the scaffold and set to work. Everything went well until Twila started to fuss and wanted out of the stroller. Robyn began talking to her from the roof, trying to distract her. Meanwhile, the church bells around Somerset County, Pennsylvania, chimed out ten in the morning.

They heard its engines roaring before they saw it. Then, coming over the hill, there it was—massive, gleaming, and gorgeous against the bright blue sky. It was so low they could see the windows and the cockpit, and it occurred to Robyn that, if the passengers were looking out, they could see her and her father working on the roof.

For Ray Stevens, an aviation buff who loves to go to airports to watch the big jets take off and land, it was a treat. He was used to seeing small planes and military jets flying over, but he didn't get to see a big jetliner that low over their little Pennsylvania valley.

"Twila, look up at the pretty plane," called Robyn, and Twila stopped fussing. But the big airliner had already disappeared over the next hill. By that time Robyn and Ray had finished the task at hand and needed a part or two. So Robyn climbed down, put Twila in the car, and set off to a store in nearby Hooversville.

• • •

Neither Robyn nor her father had turned on the television or radio that morning. If they had, they would have been mesmerized, like anyone in Somerset County who was near a television set after 9 A.M., by the spectacle of terrorists flying planes into buildings in New York City.

At the Somerset barracks of the Pennsylvania State Police, Sergeant Patrick Madigan and Lieutenant Robert Weaver, like so many in the county that morning, were watching the collapse of the Twin Towers.

"Well," sighed Madigan, "at least there are no terrorist targets in Somerset County."

• • •

Terry Butler was taking a radiator out of a car at Stoystown Auto Wreckers when someone called him on his walkie-talkie to say that a plane had flown into the World Trade Center. Butler went down to the waiting room, where there was a television, and watched until the second plane hit the Twin Towers. When he went back out to the yard, he heard that the Pentagon had also been hit. It wasn't long after that that he heard the plane coming over the wrecking yard, but he was looking in the wrong direction.

When he turned around, he saw it coming over the treetops. It was flying just a few hundred feet off the ground, improbably low for an airliner that size. Then the plane seemed to climb before making a right turn and disappearing behind the trees in the direction of Shanksville.

• • •

Linda Shepley was going out to hang clothes on the line when she heard a sound like a truck going over a bridge. She looked over her left shoulder, and there it was, close enough to see the big engines on the wings. She was used to seeing small planes coming in to the county airport, but she knew the airport couldn't take a plane of that size. And the wings were wobbling—something was terribly wrong. Should she call someone? She watched it as it descended toward Buckstown—or was it going toward Lambertsville, where her son, Michael, worked at the Rollock scrap yard?

Then all of a sudden the right wing dipped, the plane took a nosedive, and Shepley started screaming for her husband, Jim, to call 9-1-1.

At the Rollock scrap yard, work had started like any other day. Timothy Lensbouer was operating his crane when he heard over the radio that two planes had crashed into the World Trade Center in New York. Just before 10, he shut his crane off and went into the lower building to get some parts. While he was coming back up with the parts, Tim stopped in at the office to find his wife, Nena, with the crock pot she always brought so that the scrap workers would have a hot lunch. Chris Cordell, the owner's brother, who was there watching a little portable television, said that the Pentagon had also been hit and that they'd shut all the airports down.

He no sooner said that—exactly at 10:03 A.M.—than they heard a huge screaming noise, like a missile in some television show. Then the office went dark, as if a giant shadow had passed over, and they heard something like what an atomic bomb would sound like going off next door. The building shook. Chris jumped up from his chair, and he and Tim started toward the door, thinking their liquid oxygen tank had exploded.

When they threw open the door, all they could see was a column of fire down the hill that billowed more than three hundred feet in the air. A cloud of black smoke enveloped the scrap yard and everything around it. As they ran out into the yard, the scrap cutters, Michael Shepley and Lee Purbaugh, came running toward them, both terrified. They had been outdoors and had seen the thing scream over their heads—so sudden that they'd barely had time to duck— and nosedive into the earth. They were the only ones who saw it hit.

"Call 9-1-1!" Purbaugh was hollering. The plane, he said, was "one of those great big [expletives] like hit the Pentagon and the Towers this morning."

The company phones were out, but Cheryl, the secretary, was able to get through on her cell phone. By this time, Nena Lensbouer was running alongside her husband and the Rollock crew downhill

The Day the Sky Fell Down

across the trenched ground, scattered with rocks and debris. *If a plane crashed*, thought Nena, a former firefighter, *there has to be someone down there that needs help*. It seemed to take forever to get down to the crash site, even though it was only two hundred yards away. The 9-1-1 control center wouldn't let them hang up.

What do you see? they kept asking. *Tell us what you see!*

"Well, the trees are on fire. We see smoke from the ground. There's some debris hanging, like papers and stuff."

What about the plane?

"We don't see no plane."

There has to be a plane!

But there wasn't one—just a big hole in the ground that was on fire. They walked right up to the hole and looked down in it. Nothing. They hollered and screamed, but no one answered. They ran into the nearby woods, which were burning too, looking for survivors. There they found lots of scrap metal and debris, and lots and lots of paper, but no people—not even a body.

· · ·

Two and a half miles away in the village of Shanksville, assistant fire chief Rick King was talking on the phone with his sister in Lambertsville. She said she heard a plane, but King pooh-poohed it.

"No Rick. It's really loud. It sounds like a big jet." Phone in hand, King walked out on the front porch.

"Oh my God, Jody. I hear it, too," he said. Then there was a screaming noise and, seconds later, the porch shook. Like everyone else in Shanksville, King was used to hearing explosions from the mining operations, but this was way beyond that.

King didn't remember putting down the phone. He didn't remember if he closed the front door. He started running to the fire hall. When he was halfway there, the fire siren went off—someone had already called 9-1-1. King and three others who'd answered the call piled into a fire truck and screamed off down the bumpy Lambertsville Road, just a few short miles through the woods and farms, not knowing where the plane hit, but following the smoke. Thoughts of a commercial airliner with two or three hundred passengers, of fires and people trapped in fuselage, kept racing through his head. His mouth was so dry he couldn't swallow.

"Get ready guys," he said. "This is like nothing we've ever seen before."

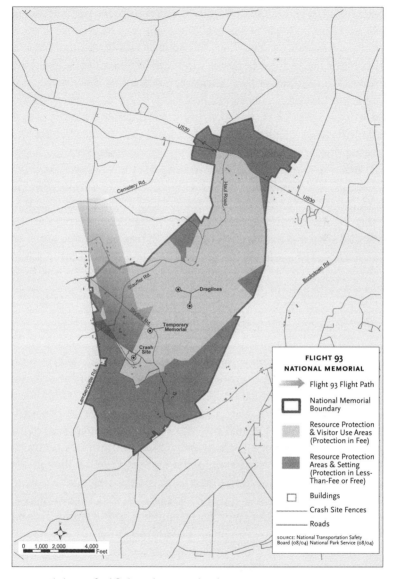

MAP 2 Flight 93's fatal flight path. National Park Service.

The Day the Sky Fell Down

At that very moment, two other firemen from nearby Stoystown, Norbert Rosenbaum and his son Mike, were also racing to the scene, their sirens wailing. They left the highway and drove up a big hill that locals called Skyline Drive, where they came upon a man on a motorcycle who yelled, "Go down this dirt road!" When Rosenbaum got down the hill that had once been an open-pit coal mine, his fire chief was already there in his pickup truck and waved him on across all the debris, straight to the fire. They put the pumper in gear and started pumping.

6

Other responders were converging on the scene—first three Pennsylvania state policemen who happened to be patrolling in the area, the county ambulance, and EMS. From then on, it seemed that every fifteen minutes somebody with a little more authority showed up, and soon the place was swarming with fire, police, and accident personnel. FBI agents from nearby Johnstown were on the scene almost immediately, followed by agents from the Pittsburgh field office, to take control of what was, as would quickly become apparent, a crime scene. Almost as quickly, legions of curiosity seekers and souvenir hunters showed up. Rick King said they should perform a search and rescue operation.

"I don't think you're going to be rescuing nobody," said Norbert.

It didn't take long for paramedic Christian Boyd to come to the same conclusion. He had raced to the site in the county ambulance from Stoystown, put on his rescue gear, and prepared to do a tri-age assessment—determine who was walking wounded, who had a pulse, who was breathing, who wasn't. He walked around seemingly forever and didn't see anybody. As he looked closer, he thought he could see the path the plane traveled from the treetops that were sheared off. With Norbert and Mike he searched back in the woods— even though the power lines were snapping and jumping around where one wing of the plane had sliced through them.

Along with the smell of jet fuel, which was overwhelming, there was another smell. Mike didn't recognize it, but Norbert, who'd been to Vietnam, did: human flesh was burning. Now Christian Boyd began to see scattered bits of human tissue throughout the woods, such as a bunch of skin that looked like something had yanked it off from the shoulder to the wrist and rolled it up in a ball. Then he looked up in the trees and saw that chunks of flesh had been catapulted up there.

There was a lot of scrap metal, but most of it you could have put in your pocket—until Norbert saw a piece the size of a car hood about thirty feet up in a tree. Among all the other debris, he and Mike found a lot of money scattered in the woods—Norbert picked up about $360 in twenty-dollar bills. When they came out of the woods, there were state troopers everywhere. Norbert walked up to one of them and handed him the wad of money. Meanwhile, dozens of souvenir hunters had converged on the site and were stuffing objects into their shirts.

Christian Boyd came upon a Bible that was burning diagonally from the corner. He didn't know how to handle it, wondering if there were some rule about this that he hadn't learned in Sunday school, so he called Mike, a devout Catholic, over. "Oh man, that's not good," said Mike, and he patted the edge of it with his hand until it went out. "I guess that's all you have to do."

When word spread about the Bible, many would see its survival amid the firestorm as a sign from God.

Mike Sube was still searching the woods with the county fire department's HAZMAT truck. It was eerily quiet. He headed toward a small pond and finally saw large pieces of wreckage, including a portion of the landing gear with one tire still attached and a piece of the fuselage with a few windows in place.

Roger Bailey, also with the county fire department, walked through the debris field. Pieces of fiberglass, pop rivets, and mail were scattered everywhere. A piece of foam rubber from a seat cushion, hardly even burned, lay near the crater. A man searching with them almost stepped on a piece of human remains and turned woozy. Roger excused him from the search.

Louis Veitz, an accident reconstruction specialist, first wondered, *Where the hell did it go? Where do you stick an airplane of that size?* But as he studied the rest of the site, he found it everywhere. When he climbed a knoll and studied the impact area, at first it seemed just a big hole in the ground, but he'd been in aircraft simulators and knew something about planes. The more he looked, the more he could see the outline of the airliner—where a wing went in, where an engine hit, where the rudder had dug into the ground as it went in. Just by looking at the scorched area from off to the side, he could tell the 757 was rolling as it came in.

▪ ▪ ▪

As reporter Jon Meyer was leaving for work at WJAC-TV in Johnstown, he was feeling good because, living in rural Pennsylvania, he and his family were safe from the terrorist attacks occurring in places like New York. So it was really strange that when he walked in the door of the television station, he received news that a plane had crashed near Shanksville, just down the highway.

He and photographer J. D. Kirkpatrick jumped into a van and sped the twenty miles to the site, expecting to find a shattered airliner and injured passengers. When they arrived, Meyer ran toward the smoke and the emergency personnel converging on the scene but found nothing except a deep crater and the powerful odor of jet fuel. He feverishly scribbled notes nearby—notes that would later prove illegible—until police and firefighters forced him back to the media barricade.

Photojournalist Sean Stipp got the call shortly after 10 A.M. from his dispatcher at the *Pittsburgh Tribune-Review*. He jumped in his car and raced the eighty miles down U.S. 30, following a caravan of police cars, turned into the scrap yard, and walked down toward the smoking crash site. He paused to shoot pictures every twenty or thirty feet until a fireman stopped him.

But even though there were no compelling images—people standing around a smoking hole wasn't exactly the same as planes flying into the Twin Towers—Stipp could sense that a mammoth event had happened here and feared that the attacks weren't over. He wasn't the only one who feared that an all-out attack on the United States was under way.

• • •

County coroner Wally Miller drove around Skyline Drive past cars parked on both sides of the road. Like so many other first responders, he seriously doubted that he was ready for what he was about to see. He'd been watching television with his father, a retired coroner, that morning. When they saw the Twin Towers collapsing, his father said, "How'd you like to be the coroner in New York City now?" Now the same calamity had struck the heart of their own rural county, and Miller was on his way to deal with it as best he could.

A tall, lanky, self-effacing man who, some thought, resembled a clean-shaven Abe Lincoln, he'd grown up with death, both in running the family funeral home and in serving as elected coroner. But murders in Somerset County were rare (Miller had only dealt with two in the course of his career), and mass murder—which is what Flight 93 turned out to be—was almost unimaginable.

As he drove toward the crash site, a more troubling question was, How many bodies was he going to find? He passed cars parked on either side of the road—hundreds and hundreds of people, many of them curiosity seekers, were already there—and parked his dark Ford Excursion as close to the crash site as he could. As he approached the firemen, he asked, "Have you seen any human remains?" Some said they had, but Miller walked the site for an hour before he saw the first recognizable body part, a piece of spinal cord with five vertebrae attached. As one firefighter put it, you knew there were people there, but you couldn't see them. Miller sensed not people but their absence—a void attesting that the passengers and crew "got snatched out of their bodies really quickly." It dawned on him that he wasn't going to be a coroner here in the sense of dealing with intact corpses. He was dealing with a huge cemetery of vaporized remains.

Things were getting unbelievably strange, he thought, like a dream or something. He couldn't believe this was happening *here*.

- - -

The first thing Robyn Blanset heard when she walked into the store in Hooversville was people talking about a plane that crashed over by Shanksville. Had anyone seen it?

"Was it a real big airliner?" asked Robyn. "I saw that flying over my house."

"Well, it might be related to what happened in New York."

"What happened in New York?" When they told her, Robyn left the store without buying anything. She drove back to where her father was, still up on the roof. "Come down, I need to talk to you," she said, knowing the news would hit him pretty hard.

"What is it? You come on up," he said.

"No, I want you to come down. You know that beautiful plane we saw? It crashed." When she added what she knew about the Twin Towers, they packed up their tools and collected Twila. That was the last work they accomplished that day.

- - -

As Shanksville pastor Robert Way drove to Skyline Drive, he was stopped by a policeman who was directing everyone out of the area. But when the officer saw his clerical collar, he said, "Pastor, would you mind going down to the crash site? They're asking for ministers to come into the area to give last rites."

Pastor Way wasn't relishing walking into that scene—"carnage" popped to mind—but that's what he'd been called to do, so he found a place to park. He immediately saw two ladies from a Buckstown church—two of the many curiosity seekers who'd immediately gravitated to the site. Could they please go down with him to the crash site? "I'm pretty sure it's something you ladies are not going to want to see," said Pastor Way. It turned out to be a moot point, because as he started down the road, he met a truckload of Shanksville men who told him to just turn around—that the FBI had declared the area a crime scene. So Pastor Way drove back to Shanksville and, just to do something that seemed normal, walked down to the post office to get the mail. While walking he noticed knots of kids standing around, in particular a group in front of Ida's Country Store.

"Is this World War III?" asked one of the kids—and another, "Are we going to die now?" Pastor Way tried to reassure them that, while the attacks in New York and Washington were indeed deliberate, the Flight 93 crash had to be an accident—there would have been no reason for anyone to crash into that field on purpose. That seemed to make sense to the kids, but Pastor Way sensed that this was the beginning of the end of life as they'd known it in their sheltered village.

At Stoystown Auto Wreckers, Terry Butler, who had seen the plane go down and had heard the explosion as it hit, went home to compose himself. After a couple of hours, he made the mistake of coming back to the wrecking yard to find the news media lined up along the highway. First was WJAC-TV from Johnstown, who interviewed him right there in the yard. Later came CNN and others—Butler lost track of all of them. Being interviewed was disorienting, with the newscasters bunched around and Butler having to stand there and answer questions with those big mikes pointing in his face.

• • •

Jason Fedok watched coroner Wally Miller walking the crash site. An expert in accident survivability with the National Transportation Safety Board in Washington, D.C., Fedok knew something about country coroners from his accident work: they had no budget, no staff, no resources. As he watched Miller, he couldn't help thinking, "He's in over his head. He just never experienced anything like this, and the poor guy's going to be on the tip of the spear until this is over."

Fedok was right that Miller had always been a one-man band as county coroner and, as such, had zero experience in leading a disaster team or delegating authority. But he did know people across the state who were in the funeral business, and he liked to work with people he knew. He called his friend, the coroner from nearby Cambria County, and told him to get there as soon as possible. And he called a forensic anthropologist from up in Erie, whom he'd worked with and who had experience with plane crashes and fragmented remains. Then a funeral director from Pittsburgh just showed up, and Miller let him stay because he had connections with the Disaster Mortuary Operational Response Team (DMORT) down in Washington, D.C. DMORT was essential because it had the sophisticated mobile equipment to deal with mass casualties and identify fragmented human remains. But others were clamoring to get involved, especially those who had had experience with the Flight 427 disaster in 1994 outside Pittsburgh, and Miller asked his father to take their calls and tell people that if he needed them, he'd call them back.

With his tiny team of colleagues and his cousin Mark, a purchasing agent at Somerset Hospital, Miller set out to deal with the huge catastrophe in front of him. He knew that he was ultimately responsible for a lot of what went on there, because if there was a deceased person on the scene in Somerset County, it was his scene. He didn't know how much control he was going to have over how it all went—for the time being the FBI was in charge of the site as a crime scene—but he knew he'd be held responsible if it *didn't* go right. He was only too well aware that the county coroner outside Pittsburgh still had lawsuits pending against him seven years after the Flight 427 disaster, because of mix-ups with remains and other issues.

"Well, this is it," Miller said to his cousin Mark. "My career is on the line, one way or the other. We're either going to see this through to a satisfactory—." He didn't finish the sentence, but he thought, "If it doesn't go right, I used to be a bartender. I guess I can go back to doing that."

In the early afternoon, Miller was called to make a media statement. He was ushered into a big car with smoked-glass windows and driven over to the media village, where the journalists were camped out and where they now circled in for a feeding frenzy. Two big tables were covered with microphones; the journalists were five deep, and each one had a tape recorder. Miller was terrified. He had always been rattled by the mere thought of speaking in public. The only time he'd been on television was the time he had to make a statement about two boys who climbed into a closet and died of smoke inhalation when the place caught fire. Now he looked over at Colonel Paul Evanko of the state police and said, "What do they want me to say? We've only been here two hours. We don't know what's going on."

"Just tell them what you know and be honest," said Evanko, so Miller just relayed the bare facts he knew and thought that would be the end of it. As he walked away from the tables, however, a woman from the *New York Times* got to him, and he tried to sum up his impressions of the crash site: "If you walked around down at the crash site, you would have thought there wasn't anybody on the plane." The *Times* reporter wound up writing a feature article on Miller, and the quote about nobody being on the plane would come back to haunt him.

"At that time, I was not media savvy," Miller would reflect later. "Not that I am now."

That afternoon Miller and his cousin Mark set out to locate X-ray and other equipment and a temporary morgue to deal with the human remains they found, in the event that DMORT took a while in sending a mobile unit or, worst case, was stretched too thin at Ground Zero and the Pentagon to come at all. Miller found a venue for his temporary morgue at the National Guard Armory, but when he returned to the crash site at about nine that night, an FBI agent yelled at him, "Where were you? You missed the six o'clock press briefing." Miller had thought he'd give one briefing that day and that was it, but it turned out that he was going to be meeting the press three times a day for at least the next month, and for a year and a half after that, he'd often take twenty calls a day from as far away as Russia. The "hick coroner," as he sometimes called himself, had become the unlikely focus of world attention.

. . .

Almost constant phone calls filled the first day at the site for law enforcement officials. Back at the Somerset barracks, Corporal William Link was manning the phones and took a call from a woman who said, "There's a woman about 150 yards in front of the impact site where the plane went down. She's still alive and she needs help!"

"How do you know that?"

"Well, I can hear her."

"Where do you live? Do you live out near the crash site?"

"No, no. I can just hear her yelling. She's yelling."

"Were you driving by? Did you have a cell? Did you stop to help?"

"No, no. I'm a psychic. I'm calling from California."

• • •

Photographer Sean Stipp's biggest impression throughout the day was of people's faces. One reporter, Rick Earl from Channel 11 News in Pittsburgh, had been a kind of role model for the young photographer. Stipp was used to seeing Rick at major warehouse fires and the like, and such events seemed just a day's work for the veteran journalist. But today, Rick Earl's face was pale, almost translucent. He wasn't talkative; he wasn't joking. And seeing faces like Rick's, it hit home for Stipp that American society, which he'd always thought so steadfast, so enduring, could really be cracked open to its core. By the end of that day at the crash site, he already had an inkling of why memorials are built and why veterans take their holidays so seriously.

• • •

Families were devastated all across America that day as the news filtered out. For Lori Guadagno, the day began in her special needs classroom in Vermont; another teacher came in to tell her that a plane had flown into the World Trade Center. Lori joined a group of students and teachers around the television in the school library, watching the first tower fall and remembering that her brother, Richard Guadagno, had an early morning flight out of Newark. He must be on the tarmac right now, she thought, seeing this right out his window.

Richard hated flying. Always had. "With my luck, I'll probably go down in a plane," he had once said. Such fatalistic nonsense drove Lori crazy.

Then the newscaster said something that made her hair stand on end: a plane from Newark to San Francisco was unaccounted for. Lori frantically called her family in New Jersey. Her father answered. "It doesn't look good, Lor," he said. "I don't know. It just doesn't look good."

Lori didn't know how she got out of the school, how she got in her car and got home. She was racking her brain for someone to call who could get definitive information and thought of her cousin Lisa in Florida, whose godfather was John Glenn. "Find the passenger list," Lori said when she finally got through to Lisa. "Call whoever you have to call in Washington. Just call." Then Lori turned on the television and gazed in horror at a smoking hole in the Pennsylvania country-side and no sign of any of the passengers. But then she thought, "I know Richard. He's so resourceful. He's so fit. He knows so many survival skills. He'll make it out." And she stared at the trees behind the crater, half expecting Richard to come walking out any minute.

Then Lisa called back. She told Lori to sit down. "I have to tell you that Richard was on that plane," she said. "It really was Richard. I'm so sorry."

The rest of the day was mostly a blur. Getting her boyfriend to come home so he could drive her to her family in New Jersey while she cried nonstop. Driving down the empty New York State Thruway and seeing signs that said, "New York City is closed." Finally reaching her parents' house and realizing that that morning, Richard had sat at their table and had breakfast. *This can't be happening to my family,* Lori told herself. *We're boring!* And watching the television and see-ing the names scrolling by, and the smoking hole again, and thinking they would all die of sadness, because how could her family go on without Richard?

. . .

Erich Bay and his wife, Lorraine, a stewardess for United Airlines, had risen very early that morning. At 4:30 Erich walked into the bathroom where Lorraine was doing her hair and said good morn-ing. "You know, sweetheart, I don't feel so good at all," Lorraine said. "I have a backache. And I have a terrible stomachache. I feel like calling in sick."

But she decided to fly anyway. At five o'clock she came by the oth-er bathroom where Erich was shaving. She squeezed his cheek and kissed him. "Goodbye, sweetheart," she said. When she got back the next day, they were going to their favorite watering hole to celebrate his birthday.

Bay got to his office in Union, New Jersey, at about 6:30 and started working on the payroll. At 8:30 an employee came in and said that a plane had just flown into the World Trade Center. Bay didn't think much about it until the second plane hit. After that he got so nervous that he couldn't add one and one. Lorraine was supposed to have taken off at 7:00, so he asked Marc, his nephew, to go to the United website and get the current flight status. But Marc came back and said, "Look, they shut down the website. You better go home."

Bay got into his car with a huge sense of foreboding. Under the blotter in his home office, Lorraine always left her flight information, and that would tell the tale. Until he lifted that blotter, there was a ray of hope. On the way home Bay stopped for gas, just to make the trip last longer. When he came in sight of his house, the whole neighborhood was in his front yard waiting for him.

• • •

In Denver, Sandra Dahl, wife of Flight 93 pilot Jason Dahl, was packing for a trip to a cabin in the Rockies when Dan Hatlestad, a neighbor, called. "Sandy, where is Jason?" he asked. "I mean, where is he right now?"

"He was in Newark last night, and by now he's on his way to San Francisco," she said. "What's going on, Dan?" He told her to turn on the television, and she watched in disbelief as one airliner slammed into the World Trade Center, then another. The second plane was from her airline, United. *These are my people*, she thought. *This can't be happening*. Then Dan called back and told her to look up Jason's status on the computer. As a flight attendant with United, Sandra was allowed to get into the company system. There she saw something that really scared her: Jason's line was blocked. That only happened when there was a crash.

Next, the newscaster said that another plane had crashed in Pennsylvania, and the images of the crash site appeared on the screen—a big, black, burning hole. Where was the airplane? Sandra had studied crashes as part of her job, but she'd never seen a black hole, ever.

The media were speculating that the Pennsylvania crash was Flight 93—Jason's flight—because all the other flights had been grounded or accounted for. Sandra began softly wailing. Then she remembered Jason's teenage son, Matt. She wanted to take him out of school before he heard anything. She called Matt's mother to say that she'd pick him up because she was closer, but Matt's mother said no, she'd get him. As soon as she hung up, Matt called—he had already been watching television with his class. "Where's Dad?" he said.

The Day the Sky Fell Down

"I don't know exactly, Matt."

"What's his flight number?"

"I don't know exactly, Matt."

"Yes, you do."

"Well, I looked it up, and it might be Flight 93," she said, and Matt started crying. Sandra went on, "Matt, that scene doesn't look right to me. I've never seen a crash site where there's no airplane. You know your dad's a good pilot. They could have crash landed. We don't know for sure." Matt was still crying, so she told him to go to the office and wait for his mother. Then Sandra tried to call someone at United, but she misdialed and got a dial-a-porn line instead. Even after dialing properly, she couldn't get through to anyone at United, so she was stuck watching television—the black burning hole—and now they were confirming that it was Flight 93.

Sandra started to cry and then went into shock, just staring at the television. Soon people began coming over to the house and talking about the crash and crying and hugging her, but she wanted to get away from that. So she walked around the side of the house and sat on the hood of her car as the house filled up. Then someone told her that she had a call from Tim Adams at United's Denver flight office.

"Sandy," he said, swallowing hard when she picked up the phone, "I have to tell you bad news."

"Is it—is it for sure?"

"It's for sure."

"Now Tim, nobody's actually been out there yet. There's just some helicopters flying over."

"We know for sure, Sandy," he said.

She got off the phone and told everyone in the house that it was official that Jason had died in the crash. Then she walked out the front door and around the side of the house, sat on the hood of the car, and just stared and stared.

• • •

Early in the morning in suburban San Diego, Deborah Borza was still at home watching news of the terrorist attacks, but wasn't worried because her daughter, Deora Bodley, a junior at Santa Clara University in California, was scheduled to take a later flight from Newark. It wasn't until she was in her office that Allie, one of Deora's friends from New Jersey, called to say that Deora had been on standby for Flight 93. Allie had dropped her off at the Newark airport in time to make the flight. Now Deborah's only hope was that Deora had been stranded at the airport when all the planes were grounded.

"Allie, do me a big favor, honey," said Borza. "See if you can get back to the airport and see if she's waiting, you know, at the terminal."

Allie called back in an hour to say that security wouldn't let her near the airport. Borza started to panic. Coworkers told her to go home, but she didn't want to go back to her empty house. Human resources brought in a trauma person who told her what to do in case the worst turned out to be true. She crossed the street to Mary, Star of the Sea Catholic Church, where several others were praying for the country and the victims of the terrorist attacks. Deborah joined them near the altar.

God, you are the only one right now who knows where she is, she prayed. *Tell me where she is.* And she heard that quiet little voice she could always count on, the voice that was always with her. *She's with me*, it said.

Borza said a short prayer to the Virgin Mary and her cell phone rang. It was a woman at United Airlines, who probably had the hardest job in the country that day, breaking the unequivocal news.

Borza dropped the phone and screamed.

People in the church hurried over. One woman asked if she'd like some water. Another offered a rosary. The priest led them in prayer, which suddenly seemed to Borza like a lot of malarkey. She called Derrill Bodley, her ex-husband, Deora's father. When Borza reached him he was on the road. "You've got to pull over," she said. When she told him the news he began yelling "No!" into the phone, and then "I've got to go. I've got to go."

• • •

That evening in Somerset County, the television began broadcasting news about the airliner. There had been forty passengers and crew on board. Good luck—if you could call it that—that the flight hadn't been full. At 8:30 P.M. President George W. Bush appeared on television to reassure a traumatized nation. "None of us will ever forget this day," he said. "Yet we will go forward to defend freedom and all that is good and just in our world."

First responder Norbert Rosenbaum was back at home in Stoystown. The full impact of what he'd witnessed really hadn't sunk in. Sure, he'd seen stuff like that in Vietnam, but he never expected to see it in Somerset County. It finally hit him around ten o'clock that night. He just couldn't move. He was paralyzed. Norbert's wife called her sister, a registered nurse, who said he was in shock.

Night descended on the site and with it a cold fog. State troopers who had been called in from low-lying parts of the state weren't prepared for the cold night at almost three thousand feet. To get them through it, local people began to bring in warm clothing and firewood.

Terry Butler, the auto wrecker, was one of those who brought supplies—paper towels and bottled water that he had bought with his own money. Butler didn't know that he, like many empathetic people in the county, would be carrying the weight of the crash on his shoulders for years to come.

• • •

Wally Miller didn't leave for home until three in the morning. His wife, Arlene, was with him. When she learned he was at the crash site, she had rushed home to bake cookies to take to him, because Miller, by his own admission, had some pretty strange eating habits. He'd been a vegetarian for twenty years, so he couldn't eat much of the food, such as hamburgers, that were hurriedly brought in for the first responders. So Arlene brought cookies to the site, and the troopers stopped her at the checkpoint and asked for official identification. She didn't have any, but she said, "I'm the coroner's wife. Do you want a cookie?" And they let her in.

She and Miller didn't talk much on the drive home because Miller was on the phone pretty much the entire time, and Arlene thought he had that deer-in-the-headlights look all the way. They decided to spend the night in of one of their two funeral homes because it was closer to the crash site and they knew they'd have to head back early the next morning.

Arlene and Miller had only been married three years, but Arlene felt that they were already about as close as two human beings could be. She didn't know too many people who could say with confidence that their marriage was unbreakable, absolutely permanent, but theirs was. She and Miller improvised a bed in the smoking lounge of the funeral home, and it turned out that this was to be their bedroom for months and months as he worked out at the site.

Before going to bed, Arlene and Miller unloaded his pockets, which were full of cards and notes and phone numbers. Both their heads were totally spinning, and when Miller lay down the events of the day seemed to pursue him into his sleep, because Arlene heard him mumbling, "Oh, Ar. Oh, Ar." That was what he called her—"Ar"—for short. "Oh, Ar. Oh, Ar," he kept mumbling, all night long.

2

IT TAKES

A VILLAGE

The village of Shanksville, Pennsylvania, has a Rip Van Winkle quality about it. After a slumber of many years, it was shaken roughly awake one September morning to discover that the world had changed around it.

Shanksville was founded as part of a wave of German immigration in the late 1700s. Even while America was still a British colony, German immigrants began settling the rich lands of what they called the Bruedersthal, or Brothers' Valley—a territory west of the Allegheny Mountains that roughly coincides with present-day Somerset County. In 1798 a German named Christian Shank cut a road to a site on the banks of the Stonycreek River, in a valley between two ridges, and built a cabin there. With him were his wife and seven sons, along with Isaac Wendel, a carpenter and millwright, and his family. They dammed the gently flowing river, gaining enough power to drive a lumber and grist mill.

Christian Shank laid out the village according to the simplest of plans—three streets parallel to the river. People began to move in, and eventually there were two blacksmith shops, a brickyard, a two-story general store, a small hotel and bar, and a dairy that shipped butter all the way to Baltimore in fifty-pound kegs. A doctor

FIG. 2   The isolated village of Shanksville nestled in its surrounding hills. Photo:
Chuck Wagner.

set up his practice in 1840. Shanksville became a self-sufficient village, known for skilled carpenters, masons, bricklayers, and other
building tradesmen. The townspeople even provided their own en-
tertainment: a 1919 photograph shows the twenty-two-piece Shanksville concert band, every musician in uniform.

Shanksville's Memorial Day parade stretched half as long as the
village, with everyone on foot. The village was decked out in red,
white, and blue. The young people went to the woods to gather ever-
greens and flowers to make wreaths, giving one to every war veteran
to place on the grave of a comrade. The people of Shanksville have
always taken good care of their cemeteries.

Since the days of the Bruedersthal, the old barn-raising ethic had
helped make the valley and its surrounding farms and woodlands a
thriving rural community. Harvesting crops and butchering livestock
were times when neighbors gathered to help neighbors. They also
knew how vital it was to help one another when crops failed, when
fires or floods wiped out homes, when men were trapped under-
ground in a mine disaster. When families were bowed down by death.

Farmers began to mine coal right on their farms in 1810, often,
again, with the help of their neighbors. The geologic strata of the

It Takes a Village

FIG. 3   Looking down Shanksville's Main Street. The village saw its last heyday in the 1970s. Photo: Chuck Wagner.

bituminous coal relative to the rise and fall of the land placed the top seams of coal near the surface in many places, and the erosion of ages had exposed the seams so that they outcropped along many hillsides and stream banks. A farmer would follow a seam into a hillside, shoring up the opening with timbers and often laying a crude wooden track on which he pushed a homemade car. When neighbors came by to pick up a wagonload of coal for their homes or forges and found the farmer working down in the mine or otherwise absent, they wrote their names and the number of bushels on a tablet that was nailed to a tree. That way, they could settle up with the farmer later. Trust among neighbors was another ethic that ran deep in the valley.

Still, the village remained a tiny borough of a few hundred people between two ridges. Probably the closest it came to serious growth was the proposed construction of a rail line in the 1880s to take advantage of the regional coal fields. Seven miles of roadbed were begun outside of town before the project was scrapped in 1885. But Shanksville remained a thriving village right up until the late 1970s, when it still enjoyed two grocery stores, a service station, an automobile dealership and garage, a doctor, a barbershop, and a modern bank.

Coal mining outside the village surged after World War II, incorporating huge draglines to strip off the soil and expose the coal underneath. On the rolling hills between Shanksville and Lincoln Highway, strip mining operations removed hundreds of thousands of tons of bituminous coal before mining out the seams, more or less replacing the soil, and shutting down operations.

The closing decades of the twentieth century were not kind to this sweet, isolated village. Family farming, the mainstay of the area, declined in the 1980s there—as it did, of course, across the rest of the United States. The ups and downs of the coal industry, the source of the best-paying jobs, also destabilized the local economy. That left only one employment center, the small local school. Residents had to commute to work far from the village, if they were lucky enough to find work at all in Somerset County, which even today has one of the least vibrant economies of any county in Pennsylvania.

Today, Shanksville has a feeling of small-town stagnation. Several houses in the village stand conspicuously vacant. The only business left on Main Street is a sandwich shop named Snida's. The bank, which closed in the 1980s, is now used for meetings of the town council, but the building is hardly ever open, because there is no paid staff. The barber shop across the street became defunct after the barber died and no one took over the business. You can't buy groceries, fill a prescription, or gas up your car anywhere in Shanksville.

The decline in family farms has been somewhat mitigated by an influx of Amish families, who bought up some farms and continue to work them. This further strengthened the historical German connection, given that the Amish still speak German with one another. You can occasionally see a black Amish horse-drawn buggy rolling down Main Street.

Whatever reverses the physical village may have suffered, however, the ethic of cooperation in the valley appears to be alive and well. The village "has a heartbeat," says Chuck Wagner, a heavy-equipment operator and lifelong resident. Wagner, like many locals, has an extended family that has chosen to stay in the area—two daughters, a son, and nine grandchildren, only one of whom has moved away from the valley. Wagner is blessed, he says, to be able to be present at the grandkids' school and sports events. Despite the relative dearth of economic opportunities, many extended families like Wagner's want to stay rooted in their home ground, in the embrace of healthy families.

Helping your neighbor is still practiced in these Pennsylvania hills, as it was in the days of the Bruedersthal. As an example of the old ethic, Wagner cites a recent benefit dinner at a local church for the family of an Amish boy who got his leg stuck in a log splitter. Another example, he says, is the dedication of the fire department, composed entirely of volunteers who undertake hard, dangerous work for no pay. The community response to Flight 93 would tap into the old values in a very serious way.

There was no denying, however, that Shanksville, at the beginning of the twenty-first century, was a sleepy hollow that had seen better days. Hardly anyone ever had a reason to visit the valley between the ridges anymore. "We kind of were not even a spot on the map," said resident Clara Hinton. "We didn't even know if we were connected, kind of, to the rest of the world." The Pennsylvania Turnpike wasn't that far away, but few outsiders ever ventured down the bumpy, winding roads that led to Shanksville.

Once in a great while, someone would relocate there to escape the hurly-burly of the outside world. Clay Mankmeyer, a retired state trooper, had moved down from Pittsburgh "to get my kids out of the city . . . and introduce them to country life, thinking that Shanksville was the perfect place to hide out."

At 10:03 that September morning, the dream of hiding out, of nestling down into the sleep of solitude, was blown asunder.

■ ■ ■

The morning after the crash, the eyes of world media turned on Shanksville, and the long parade of politicians who would appear on the Shanksville stage over the next decade began. The first to make an appearance was John Murtha, U.S. representative from Johnstown, who had flown up from Washington, D.C., that morning. As he spoke into a battery of microphones, with state troopers standing at parade rest behind him, the legend of Flight 93 was born.

"Someone here was a hero," said the white-haired, heavy-jowled Murtha to the crowd of cameramen and reporters. "A passenger or the pilot who would not fly on. There must have been a struggle. Some heroic individual brought this plane down."

Murtha was the first to publicly articulate the theme of heroism as confirmed by reports from family members. The story that gradually unfolded began with the Boeing 757 taking off from Newark International Airport, bound for San Francisco. In the passenger cabin were four Arab terrorists armed with box-cutter knives. About forty-six minutes after takeoff, they put on red bandannas, broke into the cockpit, killed or otherwise incapacitated the pilot and copilot, and assumed the controls. They swung the plane from its westerly course back toward Washington, D.C., and told the passengers that they had a bomb on board and to remain in their seats.

Had this been a conventional hijacking, the safest course would have been to remain quiet and hope that the hijackers would land the plane somewhere and eventually release the passengers. But when the passengers began calling family members from the onboard phones and cell phones, they learned that other hijacked planes had just flown into the World Trade Center and the Pentagon. The horrible truth soon became clear: they were on a suicide mission. Then a few of the passengers told their loved ones that they had taken a vote and were going to "do something"—in fact, to rush the terrorists guarding the cabin and use a food cart as a battering ram to break in.

Yes, there were brave people on that plane—but who and how many? Murtha's positing of a heroic *individual* was the first volley in a fierce debate as to whether heroism should be attributed to a single person, a small cadre, or everyone on board.

Flight 93 would prove to be extraordinarily fertile ground for the forging of legend. Because there were no survivors, no one could confirm or deny any narrative about what had happened or what the passengers were trying to accomplish. Were they actively trying to save the U.S. Capitol or some other site—or were they simply trying to get home alive? Given that ambiguity, it would prove easy to believe—and make political hay out of—the most stirring narrative. On that sunny morning of September 12, John Murtha was the first to broach such a narrative.

"I believe they fought and dove that plane into the ground," Murtha said before he boarded the helicopter back to Washington. "At some point I'm going to suggest we place a plaque out there to honor their sacrifices."

• • •

Shanksville's sudden awakening to global violence turned its world upside down. Violent crime had always been so rare in Shanksville that there was no need for a policeman or a jail. Somerset County had always dutifully sent its sons off to war, but war had never come to Somerset County. Now, with unthinkable suddenness, the strip mine outside of town had become the scene of a mass murder, and the violence of the Middle East had stamped its awful footprint on the village's doorstep.

26

"We've lost our innocence" became a common phrase around Shanksville in the wake of the crash. In the valley between the ridges, where residents were used to looking inward, the United States' long history of power politics in the Middle East, including its support of antidemocratic regimes, was not well understood. "We're not—at least I'm not—versed in world events, and religious tensions in the Middle East," said Donna Glessner, a Shanksville native who was to play important roles in the years following the crash. "And you know, for me to understand that there is this kind of evil in the world, this kind of hatred? I didn't know that kind of hatred existed."

The people of Shanksville understood some things perfectly well, however. They knew that the country had been attacked and that, in a time of crisis, the duty of all Americans is to pull together. And they knew that forty people on board that plane had somehow resisted the violence that had ripped the skies over their village, and that those people should be hailed as heroes.

• • •

The day after the crash, people in Shanksville started crafting homemade memorials.

Kim Friedline stenciled the first sign—"Shanksville Salutes the Heroes of Flight 93"—on a big piece of plywood. Problem was, Friedline lived up on the hill where no one would see the sign, so Judi Baeckel said she was welcome to put it in her yard down at the end of Main Street. Then Debbie Musser brought a wooden cross that her husband, Roger, had made and put that in Baeckel's front yard too.

By the beginning of the twenty-first century, spontaneous memorials like those in Judi Baeckel's yard had become an almost automatic response to mass disasters. At the temporary memorial for the Columbine High School shooting, a deluge of two hundred thousand items were left—personal effects, notes, signs, stuffed animals.

As many as one million items were hung on the chain-link fence surrounding the Oklahoma City bombing site.

Temporary memorials, according to American studies scholar Erika Doss, "specifically function to remember the recently, suddenly dead, to make their loss visible and public. . . . Cards and signs stating 'we will never forget' . . . suggest that the duty of memory is to acknowledge loss." In part, massive outpourings, such as those at Columbine, are made possible by the availability of cheap manufac- 27 tured items such as caps, T-shirts, and balloons, on which someone can quickly jot a heartfelt message. "The material culture of grief at sites like Columbine," according to Doss, "embodies the faith that Americans place in *things* to negotiate complex moments and events, such as traumatic death." In Shanksville, however, it is worth noting that the very first tributes were made by people's own hands.

The American flag quickly became a rallying symbol around Shanksville—and at the crash site itself. The day after the crash, state trooper Terry Wilson climbed a steep, narrow stairway seven stories up one of the rusting, decrepit draglines left over from the mining operation. After Wilson wired a flag to the top of the boom, the stars and stripes fluttered from the highest point on the site.

• • •

Because the crash site was clearly the scene of a crime, the FBI had jurisdiction over everything that went on there. But the FBI was only one of many federal, state, and county agencies that converged on the scene, including the county's Hazardous Materials Response Team, the National Transportation Safety Board, the Bureau of Alcohol, Tobacco, and Firearms, and even a United Airlines response team. Soon 1,400 people were toiling away on the site daily. Their mission: to recover and identify every item they could find—airplane parts, human remains, personal effects of the passengers and crew, and especially anything that would constitute evidence of where Flight 93 was headed and why it went down in Somerset County. The primary goal was to locate the black boxes that contained key information about the final moments of the flight and what was said in the cockpit.

An impromptu command center consisting of prefab buildings, trailers, and tents crammed with investigative equipment and high-tech communications was assembled with amazing speed. The Pennsylvania Department of Transportation even paved a road down to the crash site. Only authorized personnel were allowed in the perimeter of the crime scene area. Even the press was consigned to a "village" on the other side of the hill.

In those first days after the crash, little was known about exactly how the plane went down and where the black boxes might be found. Investigators were at first unaware that so much of the huge airliner had been swallowed up by the relatively small crater. Some thought that the force of the explosion had blown the black boxes into the nearby woods or beyond, into Indian Lake, a resort and golf club a mile and a half from the crash site.

To solve the mystery, hundreds of investigators would scour the site for thirteen days. Anyone entering the innermost perimeter of the crash site had to don a HAZMAT suit for fear that the terrorists had contaminated the site with biological agents. About 150 agents in yellow HAZMAT suits combed the crater, the woods, and nearby Indian Lake. They fanned out over the site, hundreds of them. They got down on their hands and knees and went through the impact area hundreds of times, sometimes sifting through the dirt with their hands. They drained a pond in the hemlock trees looking for aircraft parts.

Combing the ground around the crater was a brutal exercise, if only because the searchers were constantly reminded of what the passengers went through in those last terrible moments. At least one agent doubted that he'd ever be able to set foot on an airplane again.

As accident reconstruction specialist Louis Veitz spent more time in the crater, he unearthed personal belongings and started to imagine those who had owned them. Digging up a shoe or a piece of jewelry made him feel terrible, but he'd try to concentrate on the task at hand—until he found the next piece of clothing or a pocketbook with family pictures in it. His team located very little in the way of recognizable remains, but they did find the occasional part of a limb and, finally, a person's face. Just a face.

Not all the body fragments were on the ground—some had been lobbed up in the hemlocks by the impact of the explosion. Arborists Mark Trautman and Ben Haupt were brought in from State College to scale the hemlocks using spiked boots and set ropes and retrieve whatever body parts were up there. It was perhaps the most surreal task on a surreal site. The woods were eerily quiet, and the smell of burned jet fuel, charred plastic, and human remains was horrendous. Trautman would have to throw away his favorite pair of climbing boots after he got home—the smell just wouldn't go away.

On the first day, Haupt came upon some pretty large remains up in the treetops, and he broke down. Then Trautman found somebody's buttocks, and a foot with only three toes on it. But the arborists didn't retrieve all the remains from the canopy—a flock of crows got to them first.

All human remains, however fragmentary, ended up at the temporary morgue at the National Guard Armory. The responsibility for identifying the remains fell primarily to the Disaster Mortuary Operational Response Team (DMORT), which was created in the 1980s specifically to respond to the death toll of modern mass disasters.

In charge of the DMORT morgue operation was forensic anthropologist Paul Sledzik. With a background in identifying bone specimens of Civil War soldiers, he had worked with DMORT to identify human remains after the Oklahoma City bombing. Driving up from Washington, D.C., after the disaster, Sledzik was nervous. His mentors and supervisors were mainly embroiled in the huge death toll at Ground Zero, and as head of a team of forensic technicians in Shanksville, he was going to be pretty much on his own. Even though he had led investigative teams before, this assignment was daunting.

The single goal of the DMORT team at the crash site was to identify the victims, or what was left of them. The remains were brought into the armory in a plastic bin and laid out on a counter, then sorted in a triage system: Which remains had the greatest potential for positive identification? They could be a knee, an ankle, or a hand, but they were so discolored and mixed in with nonhuman debris that it took considerable expertise to identify them. Personal effects such as a ring would go into a personal effects flow, but if the ring was on a finger, that ring would stay with the hand.

The piece of human tissue would then pass through a kind of assembly line in which it would be photographed, X-rayed, and subjected to multiple tests with scientific instruments. Fingers had potential for fingerprint identification, teeth or jaw fragments had potential for dental identification, and any hardware, such as hip replacements, could be compared against a database of identifying characteristics, many of which were provided by the victims' families.

Most fragments were untraceable without sophisticated testing, but sometimes a fragment showed up that was all too recognizable. State trooper James Broderick was working security at the temporary morgue, where he would help unload the bins of body fragments so that the analysts could sort through them. One day an analyst reached into the bin and pulled out a piece of flesh—charred, but clearly bearing a Superman tattoo. It was small enough to fit in Broderick's hand, but the red, yellow, and blue logo with the "S" in it was clear as day. And Broderick recalled seeing a photo of one of the passengers, Louis Nacke, on television with that superman tattoo on his arm. For better or for worse, the family would at least get back *something* they could recognize of their loved one.

The armory building was stifling. There was no air conditioning—just the doors propped open and fans blowing—and the smell of decaying remains was intense. Personnel were working seven days a week, from early in the morning until late at night. The pressure took its toll on everyone, including Sledzik.

Three or four days into his two-week stint in the morgue, Sledzik felt a need to reach out to the national DMORT team commander, who had trained him and was now toiling away at Ground Zero. Sledzik just wanted the commander to say, "You guys are doing okay. It's going to be fine." But when Sledzik reached him on the phone, the commander said he didn't have time and would call back later.

Sledzik walked out behind the morgue, sat down, and cried for fifteen minutes. Finally, he wiped his eyes and told himself that his team had a job to do and they'd get through this. And he walked into the armory and back to his work at the morgue tables. In the end, his team processed approximately 1,500 tissue specimens and made 500 positive identifications.

• • •

Meanwhile, the FBI had hired local excavators, including Chuck Wagner, to dig down into the crater, and on Thursday they unearthed the flight data recorder, which records an aircraft's speed, altitude, position, and other information. But investigators were much more anxious to find the cockpit voice recorder, because it could have picked up conversations in the cockpit and even some sounds from the passenger cabin.

They kept digging, and at 8:25 p.m. that Friday, they found it, twenty-five feet below where they had found the other recorder—a tribute to the violence of the impact. They immediately flew it to the National Transportation Safety Board offices in Washington, which confirmed that the passengers had, in fact, launched a revolt and were breaking into the cockpit or were actually inside it when the airliner went down.

• • •

On Saturday, the U.S. senators from Pennsylvania, Rick Santorum and Arlen Specter, flew to the site to donate the flag that had flown over the U.S. Capitol on September 11. They joined in a prayer service at the impromptu memorial led by a rabbi, a Catholic priest, and a Baptist minister.

"Let me say to the world: Terrorism will never defeat the American spirit," said Reverend Russ Kessler of Somerset, a former marine. "God is going to use this tragedy in a very unique and special way to revive America."

Less superpatriotic was the message offered by Rabbi Ronald Bluming of Johnstown, who recited the Hebrew prayer for the dead, though he was moved to tears before finishing. Bluming later said, "You cannot grasp the impact of terrorism. Israel has been dealing with this for years, but we've been shielded. But no more."

When Specter took the microphone, he raised the issue of heroism and advocated awarding the Freedom Medal to those on board the plan—some of them, anyway—who may have saved the Capitol and members of Congress, including Santorum and himself. The senators thought, however, that just three out of the forty passengers—Jeremy Glick, Tom Burnett, and Mark Bingham—deserved the medal. Specter went on, "Jeremy Glick was reported to have told his wife that he was going to take action—a strong guy, a tough guy—and all the indicators are that they rushed the pilot and they brought the plane down."

The list of "true" heroes had swelled from John Murtha's one to three, but whatever the number, the senators' proposal for this highest of civilian honors would go nowhere in Congress. Subsequent proposals for national medals would likewise languish. It would take a full decade for any sort of national award to be forthcoming, and then only in a much-diluted form.

As patriotic Pennsylvanians banded together to show their solidarity with all Americans against the terrorist threat, patriotism swelled to proportions never before seen in Somerset County, most visibly in the in-your-face display of the American flag. At Jennerstown Speedway, about six miles from the crash site, scores of volunteers unfurled a seven-ton flag the size of a football field in preparation for a rally on the Monday night following the crash.

"I want to send a message to our enemy," said the flag's owner, Ted Dorfman of nearby Greensburg, who had bought the flag and had it trucked in from Kansas. "I want to let them know that they've blown us out of our offices and killed our people and taken innocent lives, but we will continue to have babies, we will return to our jobs, and we will travel at will. The American flag will speak for itself."

• • •

In this sleepy hollow that outsiders hardly ever visited, there were now media personnel swarming everywhere. It got so that when Pastor Way left the church office and walked down to the post office, a car would stop and a reporter would jump out and ask, "Can I talk to you for a minute, Pastor?" It started to feel like harassment, and Pastor Way began driving the short distance to the post office and refusing reporters who called to ask foolish questions.

"How do your parishioners feel?"

"How do you think they feel?" asked Pastor Way. "A plane fell in their backyard. They are scared. They are worried about what will happen next."

Pastor Way delivered a sermon the first Sunday after 9/11 in a charged atmosphere. Attendance was way up—even people who didn't generally attend church were there. But Pastor Way had struggled composing the sermon. Anger at the Middle Eastern terrorists who had done this was almost palpable around Shanksville. One man at the end of Lambertsville Road had put up a banner outside his house that read "Kill Them All."

Pastor Way stood up in church that Sunday and spoke against such hatred. "Don't let this evil act turn to evil within us," he said. "Our faith says that we meet evil with acts of love, even as we ask forgiveness for ourselves. We all fall short of the glory of God." But this wasn't a message everyone in the congregation wanted to hear. Pastor Way didn't get so many of the usual "Good sermon, Pastor" comments as parishioners filed out.

Like most Americans, Somerset County residents were reeling from the loss of their sense of invulnerability, the realization that the mighty oceans were no longer a moat against the world's violence. Pastor Ed DeVore in nearby Friedens, however, had his own perspective on his neighbors' rude awakening. He'd been to Kenya with his church and had seen the hardships that people there dealt with every day. The crash had just brought home to Somerset County what much of humanity experiences almost routinely.

To Pastor DeVore, some responses to the disaster seemed a little bizarre. That first week, a woman called from the group Good Bears of the World, which sends teddy bears to traumatized communities. Could the crash site, she asked, use some teddies? Pastor DeVore told the woman to send the bears, even though he doubted that teddy bears would do much to mitigate the murder of forty people.

And yet teddy bears had recently become the universal mascot for mass tragedies in America. In Oklahoma City, where a daycare center was devastated by the bombing, the city ran out of people to give them to. Teddy bears were arguably out of place at the Flight 93 site, given that there were no children on the flight. And at least one commentator felt that they trivialized the deaths and shielded the public from the ugly reality of how and why people died. Nevertheless, stuffed bears would be one of the tributes routinely left at the temporary memorial.

Immediately after the crash, people started coming to the site to leave tributes—flowers, wreaths, little American flags, and personal items with handwritten messages. They came from all over Pennsylvania, then from nearby states, then from all over the country, and soon from around the world. The tributes were coming in so fast in the first week that local people realized that they needed a place to accommodate them.

So they built an impromptu memorial out of straw contributed by a local dairy farmer. They tiered it like an altar and made it look as tidy as a straw bale can look. Pretty soon you couldn't see the straw anymore, so fast were the stuffed animals and candles and other tributes being left there. The altar had to be expanded three times, until it was thirty feet long. A local church erected a rustic cro ss nearby.

Pennsylvania Lieutenant Governor Mark Schweiker visited the site a week after the crash and was overcome. He had just visited the straw-bale memorial before sitting down with reporters. One of them asked how the state's response to the crash differed from responses to mine disasters and other crises, and Schweiker broke down. "I wish we could have done more. I wish we could have done more," he said. "It was so final last Tuesday. When you respond to a flood or a tornado . . . there are mechanical things you can do quickly. . . . Often you can save people." But with Flight 93, the futility of any rescue effort left many, like him, despondent.

Even hardened reporters were affected. Even though they were headquartered at a "media village" over the hill and were not allowed to visit the crater, they could see the faces of those who worked around the crater and feel the pall that hung over the whole area. Reporter Sherry Stalley felt that every journalist who worked at the scene "lost it" at some point. "You would see a photographer put a camera down right in the middle of an interview. That is unheard of," she recalled. The photographer would "walk away and then come back a half hour later. You knew they had been crying."

• • •

On the Monday following the crash, a caravan of buses drove down a mountain road. In a visit coordinated by United Airlines and the American Red Cross, bereaved families had come to Somerset County to see for themselves the place where their loved ones had come to ground. They came in two shifts, the second coming the following Thursday—a total of 240 family members.

At Seven Springs Mountain Resort, where they stayed, a room had been set up with folding panels so that the parents of the victims could give blood for DNA testing to help identify pieces of tissue. The families also had to bring combs, toothbrushes, hairbrushes, and other personal effects of their loved ones for DNA sampling. To family member Gordie Felt, whose brother Edward had died in the crash, it all seemed "just gruesome."

Wally Miller came over and met about a third of the family members at Seven Springs, even though the Red Cross didn't want him there because talking to a funeral director would be "too traumatic." Instead, the Red Cross had brought in counselors to shepherd family members around.

"I don't know how many coroners' cases they've worked," Miller would say, "but I've worked a lot of them, and I know, when somebody's killed out on the Turnpike and family comes in, they don't want to talk to a mental health counselor. They want to know, Where's my son? Where's his stuff? Can I see him? What do I do next? There's no mental health counselor that's going to tell you that."

So, over the Red Cross's protestations, Miller met with as many next of kin as he could—and, indeed, what most wanted to know was, "Where are my loved one's remains and how am I getting them back?" Miller knew that none of them were going to get what they wanted. They wanted to view their loved ones, but nobody was going to get a full set of remains.

Despite the efforts to comfort the families by surrounding them with counselors and airline company volunteers, family members often told Miller, "I wish they would just leave me alone. Every time I turn around they're asking me how I feel. How do they think I feel? I just lost someone I love."

At Seven Springs, grieving families first set eyes on other grieving families. For Barbara Catuzzi, the mother of passenger Lauren Grandcolas, rubbing shoulders was "brutal": "All these strangers. We had this terrible thing in common. We all wanted to hug each other, but we didn't know who they were." Then Catuzzi and her husband, Larry, met Esther Heymann and Ben Wainio, parents of Honor Elizabeth Wainio, who had been sitting next to Lauren on the flight. Lauren had lent Honor Elizabeth her cell phone so that she could make her last call home. Larry and Barbara hugged Esther, who was an emotional wreck, as they all were. Family members were crying so constantly that staff gave out bottles of water to ward off dehydration.

Those family members who could bear it boarded buses and headed down the mountain. The bus ride began in tense silence. Everyone on board knew that they were going to see the mass grave of their loved ones. Allison Vadhan of Atlantic Beach, New York, whose mother, Kristin White-Gould, had died in the crash, was on one of the buses. She hadn't wanted to come. What was the point of going to Pennsylvania just to stare down into a hole? But friends convinced her that if she didn't go, she'd regret it someday. So here she was, on the bus with other families of the victims, rolling through the Somerset County countryside. Then they started seeing signs and American flags on the country roads, hill after hill, and signs that read "Thank You," "God Bless America," and "Never Forget."

The caravan rolled into Shanksville. The tiny village was adorned with red, white, and blue wreaths and flags hanging out of windows or on fences. A church group was there with a big, folded American flag, and dozens of residents gathered between houses. One of them was Judi Baeckel, who had put that homemade sign in her yard the day after the crash. Now she stood in her front yard just to show support.

When the buses began to weave their way through the village's narrow streets, lots of people waved, but Baeckel thought that waving might not be appropriate. So she stood with her hand over her heart, because her heart was breaking for the families. She wanted to reach out to them, but she couldn't. The windows on the buses were dark, and she could hardly see anyone, but when she saw someone wave, she waved back. Or somebody would blow a kiss, and she'd blow a kiss back. Whatever she saw them do, she did. But mostly she just stood there with her hand over her heart.

Then the locals unfurled the big flag, and a Shanksville woman started singing "Amazing Grace." Plenty of people were crying. In that moment, a bond seemed to form between the bereaved families and the people of Shanksville. *We are with you in your sorrow,* the locals' eyes and waving hands seemed to say. *We will stand by you for as long as it takes, for whatever you need to make it through this.*

Indeed, the families' plight had touched something very deep in the people of this isolated village. In today's fast-paced mall and freeway culture, which seems to define much of America, it is easy to be cynical about being your brother's keeper. But in this particular Pennsylvania heartland, that old Bruedersthal ethic of standing by your neighbor is alive and well.

State troopers and other personnel were waiting for the buses at the crash site. One of them was Frank Monaco, a major with the state police, who felt absolute awe for the people on the plane. To him, they were the true American royalty. Not the Kennedys or pop stars or rich people, but people who, under the most difficult circumstances, made the kind of choice they made. They knew what was going to happen, yet they stood up and fought. And that, for Monaco, was the true American spirit: You don't go down like sheep. Against all odds, you stand and fight.

Monaco wanted to show respect for the families, for their loss and what their loved ones did. So he came up with the idea of all the state police at the site saluting them when they rolled onto the crash site. The idea immediately caught on, even though the troopers were suffering from lack of sleep. When the buses turned onto the gravel road leading to the ominous field, hundreds of state troopers were lined up along the road like a gauntlet. They snapped to attention, and the buses rolled those last hundred yards between their salutes.

The families couldn't see it, but many of the troopers had tears in their eyes.

As the families stepped down from the buses, volunteers gave them roses, along with flat Styrofoam angels inscribed with the words "Someone prayed for you today," crafted by members of a local church congregation.

Glenn Kashurba, a Somerset psychiatrist, was on one of the buses as a Red Cross volunteer and watched some of the families follow a fluorescent orange fence down to the crash site.

"The impact point," Kashurba later wrote, "looked like a construction project with the workers on break. Large piles of dirt and heavy equipment stood around a large hole. Charred trees at the edge of a forest provided the background. . . . Stillness and silence radiated from the crater. The families replied with muffled sobs and louder cries of grief.

"The Red Cross counselors backed away and allowed the families to do whatever they needed to do with their time at the site. . . . For the next ninety minutes, FBI, State Police and NTSB officials circulated among the families, answering questions. Clergy prayed with small groups of mourners. Some families took pictures. Others just stared at the crater."

It was hard for Frank Monaco to watch the families openly grieve. It was, he thought, like going to a funeral home when there has been an unexpected death and the family is in pieces. Except that here there were forty families.

Not every family member grieved the same way. Allison Vadhan, who hadn't wanted to come, didn't cry at all at the site. In fact, she didn't cry until Christmas. On this visit she was still in shock and knew that if she started crying, she wouldn't be able to stop. But this didn't stop her from finding her way to the straw-bale memorial and leaving roses and a photo of her mother holding Vadhan's baby, with a note telling her mother that she loved her more than she'd ever know.

Jack Grandcolas of California, whose pregnant wife, Lauren, had died in the crash, had been on one of the buses too. When they arrived, he climbed a hill, looked down on the crash site, and was struck by its serenity. It wasn't like the horrifics of Ground Zero, all twisted steel and dust. It was a beautiful field.

Grandcolas then walked to a more private area away from family members milling around and crying. He had brought with him a Dictaphone with a recording of Lauren's last phone message to him from the plane. He turned on the Dictaphone and began recording his own message.

"Honey, I'm here now," he said. "I'm with you as much as I can be, at the spot where you were laid to rest." He cried and told her how much he missed her. He then archived the message. Just as others would come together to plan and build an official memorial for the passengers and crew, Grandcolas's Dictaphone archive would constitute his own personal memorial, which he says will stay with him until the day he dies.

The families lingered for nearly an hour at the crash site before traveling the mile and a half to Indian Lake Resort, where First Lady Laura Bush and Pennsylvania governor Tom Ridge were on hand to lead a more formal memorial service. It took place under a one-hundred-foot-long white tent on a golf course fairway, out of sight of the recovery operations, but the hills surrounding the crash site served as a backdrop.

"We cannot ease the pain, but this country stands by you," Bush told an audience of families, most of whom remained composed. "We will always remember what happened that day, and to whom it happened." She quoted a line of poetry: "Love knows not its own depths until the hour of parting."

Bush later told reporters that she was struck by the fact that none of the surviving relatives and friends made any suggestion that military revenge would be balm for their emotional wounds. Nonetheless, exactly three weeks later, U.S. aircraft would begin raining bombs on Afghanistan.

Back at Seven Springs Mountain Resort that evening, reporters asked for statements from family members. Most were too lost in their own grief to oblige, but Gordie Felt stepped forward. Asked whether the visit provided him, his mother, and another brother with closure, Felt said, "It's a start. I don't know what will bring total closure. It was probably the first of many visits needed to bring closure." Few family members could imagine how elusive that wished-for closure would prove to be.

Felt told reporters that *everyone* on the plane was a hero for overpowering the hijackers to save others. In a few short days, then, the estimate of heroes on board had swelled from one, according to John Murtha, to all of the passengers and crew. Of the crash site itself, Felt said, "I consider it hallowed ground. When you think of it, it was our first victory against the terrorist threat."

• • •

If the crash site was hallowed ground, what kind of marker would proclaim this? Vernon Spangler, the farmer who used to own the land before it was mined, found what had happened on his former homestead "traumatic" but said, "A memorial—definitely, definitely, there has to be one." But what kind of memorial did this terrible event seem to demand?

Cultural geographer Kenneth Foote has studied sites of mass tragedy and documented three outcomes for such places.

Obliteration is a common fate for sites of mass murder, when the fatal event is thought too terrible or shameful to warrant being remembered in any physical form. For example, the Milwaukee apartment building where serial killer Jeffrey Dahmer murdered his victims has since been demolished.

Designated sites are those that communities wish to remember but not necessarily glorify. If individuals have died in a given event, their deaths do not illustrate any sacrifice for a principle, nor is the event a historical turning point for the community. Erecting a modest sign or marker is usually considered sufficient physical commemoration. At the Flight 93 site, John Murtha's suggestion of "a plaque out there to honor their sacrifices" pointed squarely in the direction of designation.

Sanctification, the most exalted form of commemoration, occurs when the tragic site marks a turning point in the life of the community or the nation, or is where a hero or heroes made a sacrifice that embodies some moral victory that transcends their deaths. Such sites constitute "hallowed ground" and require the creation of a "sacred" space set apart from its surroundings. A sanctified site is likely to warrant a professionally designed memorial dedicated in a formal ceremony and to be the focus of regular commemorative rituals. Very few sites, Foote discovered, rise to the level of sanctification. Historically, sites of mass murder have almost never been accorded that honor.

The Oklahoma City bombing changed all that. Suddenly, the site of a hideous mass murder—a perfect candidate for obliteration—became the site of a massive effort at sanctification. It is difficult to piece together why this reversal of hierarchy took place. The usual criteria for sanctification—heroes making a sacrifice that embodies a moral victory transcending their deaths—did not apply in the pointless waste of life that was the bombing of the Murrah Federal Building. Nor did the bombing mark a turning point in the life of the community or the nation, except in a very malignant sense.

40   Yet the community of Oklahoma City came together to sponsor and build a magnificent memorial to the horror at a total cost of $29 million. The president of the United States presided at the inaugural. Yearly commemorative events are still held there.

The elapsed time for the building of memorials also changed with Oklahoma City. Historically, proposals for memorials could languish for decades. The University of Texas, for instance, was the site of a mass murder in 1966, but the university waited until 1999—a thirty-three-year delay—to dedicate a small memorial garden to the victims. Oklahoma City, however, planned, funded, and built its memorial in a whirlwind five years. The Flight 93 site seemed a likely candidate for, if anything, an even speedier memorial process. The opposite turned out to be true.

Still, it was becoming clear that a grateful nation would demand that an official memorial be placed where the hero or heroes went down. But what would finally be built in this seared and stricken place? Would it be "a plaque out there to honor their sacrifices" or something more sublime? Would its path to construction and dedication be smooth and dignified, as befitting this solemn place, or fraught with conflict? And when the definitive memorial was built, would there still be room in Somerset County for unofficial memorials—straw bale or otherwise—to that tragic day?

• • •

FBI agent Todd McCall passed a little elementary school every day as he drove to the crash site from his hotel in Somerset, the county seat. The first day he passed it, there was an American flag or two hand-painted on the front window of the school. The second day there were a few more, and by the third or fourth day every window in the building was covered by hand-painted American flags. Seeing those every day touched McCall—a twenty-year FBI veteran who had also investigated the Oklahoma City bombing—very deeply.

Now it was time for McCall to go home. The FBI had investigated the crash site for nearly two weeks and was turning it over to coroner Wally Miller, who would henceforth decide what could and could not be done there. On the last day McCall drove down the county road, he made a point of stopping at the school and walking into the principal's office. He told her that he just wanted to say thanks—that seeing those flags had strengthened his dedication at the crash site every day.

"Could you stand here for a minute?" asked the principal, and she picked up the microphone for the intercom system and said she had someone special with her. Then she handed McCall the microphone.

"Boys and girls, teachers, I just want to say thanks," McCall began. "I'm one of the agents that's working out here where Flight 93 crashed, and your flags have meant a lot to all of us." Then he had to stop, because his voice was starting to crack, and an FBI agent can't let that happen to him. So he just said, "Thanks," handed the microphone back to the principal, and stepped out into the hall to leave. But before he could make it two steps, every classroom door in the building opened up and kids started flooding out and applauding.

We'll survive, thought McCall as he stood there in the hallway. *We can take the shot and we'll survive.* And he hoped the kids realized it too.

3

THIS HARVEST
OF SORROW

On September 20, 2001, a grim and resolute President Bush stood on the podium in the House of Representatives during a joint session of Congress. Just nine days after the attacks, the president had come to this chamber to declare a War on Terror before a national television audience. Speaking in measured, deliberate tones, he spoke of the wrong done to America and vowed to use the full might of the U.S. military to avenge the worst-ever attacks on American soil.

Sitting near the front of the chamber was a petite blond four and a half months pregnant, wearing a black dress. At the beginning of his speech, President Bush asked Congress to recognize her, the wife of "an exceptional man named Todd Beamer," who "rushed terrorists to save others on the ground." Bush didn't have to add any more details—virtually every American by then knew that Todd Beamer was the passenger whose phrase "Let's roll" was thought to have launched the passenger revolt. Lisa Beamer got a standing ovation from both houses of Congress.

Todd Beamer's posthumous fame had catapulted his widow to instant celebrity. The Bush team had picked her—*not only out of all the Flight 93 families, but out of all the family members of all the 9/11 attacks*—for this extraordinary prominence. And not just the Bush team. Lisa had already been in New York for interviews on national television networks with Stone Phillips, Diane Sawyer, and Larry King.

Why did the media and the president focus on *just one* family member rather than a representative sampling of all the families? According to Cynthia Weber, a scholar of international relations who hails from a Pennsylvania town just fifty-six miles from the crash site, the shaken American public needed an "action hero" through whom they could find their collective purpose. Todd Beamer became that iconic figure. That he was a fallen hero was, in a way, convenient: no one could confirm or deny the purpose President Bush attributed to him—to save the lives of Americans on the ground.

But with no living hero to whom the American people could look, says Weber, Lisa Beamer became necessary, as the "patriotic wife and mother whose personal loss of her husband was something Americans . . . seemed to understand as a necessary sacrifice for the nation." Not least, Lisa was attractive in a wholesome, middle-American way. Her poise in the face of tragedy, her willingness to talk about her husband, and her faith in God seemed to reassure television viewers who were traumatized by the events of September 11.

Hers was to be a very public grief. Beamer made two hundred media appearances within the first six months after 9/11, appearing on *60 Minutes*, *20/20*, and *Oprah*, and again on *Larry King Live*, among other programs. She was featured in the *New York Post*, *Time*, and *Newsweek*. *People* magazine selected her as one of the twenty-five most intriguing people of 2001. In November she hired a New York publicist to manage her schedule. When she gave birth to Todd's baby in January, the event would be heralded in more than two hundred newspapers nationwide. In 2002 she would work with a professional writer to publish the inspirational book *Let's Roll!*

Some Flight 93 family members resented the disproportionate attention given to Lisa Beamer. Private remarks and letters to the editor in periodicals demonstrated that her unique celebrity had sparked envy among Flight 93 families who did not share her fame. The widespread perception of Todd Beamer as the preeminent onboard actor "divided other families, previously unknown to each other, who had been united by their suffering," according to journalist Jere Longman, who interviewed all the families shortly after 9/11.

"Resentment sprung from inconsolable grief and scattershot anger. Bitterness welled in the perception that passengers aboard Flight 93 had attained unequal status in their deaths."

. . .

Despite all the attention to the passengers' bravery, the Flight 93 crash site was not drawing the same intense media coverage as Ground Zero. The *Washington Post* called Flight 93 "September 11's forgotten flight." It wasn't just that the death toll was so much lower or that no national symbols had been smashed; more telling from a media perspective, there were no good images to engage the audience. Jim Oliver, editor of Somerset's *Daily American*, contrasted the Flight 93 site with the riveting images of Ground Zero, noting, "Here, the best pictures were a bunch of guys standing around a hole."

And yet people were starting to find their way to the crash site. They came from increasingly distant parts of the country, despite the lack of signage and the need to navigate a maze of winding country roads. Not that there was much to see once you got there— just a blank and featureless field. The only real focal point was the straw-bale memorial. And yet the visitors flooded the rustic altar with tributes: votive candles, flowers and wreaths, caps, ceramic angels, and notes. Handwritten, heartbroken notes. They planted flags in the straw bales. Somebody erected a wooden cross.

The county government wasn't sure what to do with it all. How long would people keep leaving tributes? Once the bad weather started, would people stop coming? The county leaders called a meeting one month after the crash and determined that they needed to manage the site. They asked Barbara Black, a trained curator at the Somerset Historical Society who happened to live in Shanksville, to collect and catalog the straw-bale tributes.

Black had never dealt with objects like these, beneath the notice of most self-respecting museum curators. Objects held together with duct tape. Candles, melted by the sun all over nearby offerings. Anything red, white, and blue, even the most banal consumer knickknacks. But these frail materials, Black believed, were sending strong, heartfelt messages. And some of the objects seemed to have hidden meanings. What, for example, did baby shoes left at the memorial mean, given that no children were on the plane? Black could only speculate.

At the Historical Society, she treated each item, however mundane, as if it were unique and irreplaceable. She dried the object, cleaned it using conservation methods, described and photographed it, catalogued it, and assigned it a number so that she could track it. The sheer volume of tributes soon overwhelmed the Historical Society; they were shipped to a secure government facility in Butler, Pennsylvania—again, as if they were one-of-a-kind artifacts.

Despite Black's dogged persistence, it was quickly becoming obvious that the county had neither the resources to manage the site, with its flood of tributes and visitors, nor the capacity to begin thinking about a memorial. Federal involvement was needed, and Congressman Murtha from Johnstown stepped in. He had a good working relationship with the National Park Service (NPS) through its parks in western Pennsylvania and felt that the NPS—guardian of the nation's memories through its stewardship of memorials and historic sites—was the proper federal agency to get involved. When he asked the NPS to assist Somerset County in whatever way was needed, he set the stage for much of what would happen going forward.

. . .

Coroner Wally Miller drove up to the crash site each day. He'd hit the siren on his Ford Excursion to alert the troopers that he was entering the restricted area. As coroner, he had control of what he regarded as a cemetery and therefore sacred ground, but only after the FBI had scoured the site for evidence for thirteen days.

During the entire time FBI agents had combed the site, they had found fewer than six hundred pounds of certified human remains. Wally Miller made a grim calculation: if the combined weight of the forty-four people on board was roughly seven thousand pounds, that meant that 92 percent of their remains could never be extricated from the site. The place was always going to be a mass grave.

By now the "hick coroner" had become the spokesman for the crash site, fielding numerous interviews, which took up three or four hours a day. The hardest part was telling the same story over and over and over, because the investigation didn't evolve much—it was just the same recovery protocols day after day. Miller found the media hoopla annoying and distracting, because he saw his role as simply being there for the Flight 93 families.

The coroner who handled the Flight 427 crash near Pittsburgh in 1994 advised him to keep his distance from the families—that

FIG. 4 Wally Miller, Somerset County coroner, meets with Ben Wainio and Esther Heymann at the crash site. Photo: *Johnstown Tribune-Democrat* (Mike Faher).

contact about this volatile topic could only mean trouble. "That's not what I do," said Miller. "I will talk to them. If they don't like what I'm doing, they can tell me. If they want to ask hard questions, I will give them hard answers as to what's going on so they will not feel like they are being left out of it." When it was all over, he wanted families to walk away from Somerset County knowing there were people there who cared about them.

"I wanted the world to realize we are what we are," he said. "We might be hicks, but we're hicks who know what compassion is."

So Miller made it his mission to contact the families of each victim. Not all wanted to talk to him, much less journey to Shanksville to meet him on the hillside overlooking the crash site. Others, however, made the trip, hoping that Miller could help them understand what had happened to their loved ones. Ultimately, there would be hundreds of face-to-face meetings on that hillside.

Miller maintained strict custody of the impact site, rebuffing requests for unofficial access. "I wanted to get the mindset early on that this was not a place where you just wanted to be down there stomping around hunting artifacts," he said. "Because it was a cemetery. The vast majority of the remains were vaporized down there."

Even when superstar news anchor Katie Couric showed up with a camera crew, wanting to film directly on the crash site, Miller refused.

"Lisa Beamer said it's okay," said Couric.

"Lisa Beamer doesn't speak for all the families and I'm not letting you walk on the site. You can walk over there, but *this* is sacred, hallowed ground."

The aftermath of the crash consumed Miller for months. He worked far beyond the hours that could be reasonably expected of a part-time county coroner. His phone never stopped ringing, and the unending grind of eighteen-hour days was wearing him out. "He's tired, very tired," said his wife, Arlene, who filled in as an unpaid deputy, taking months of unpaid leave from her job to deal with the mass of paperwork related to the crash. Under the circumstances, she figured that Miller's $35,854 salary as coroner amounted to "something like forty cents an hour."

Meanwhile, the long, painstaking process of identifying the fragments of the victims (by their DNA or, in some cases, fingerprints) was moving forward under Miller's direction. One night he got a call at 4 A.M.—from Beirut, Lebanon. The man on the line said he was the uncle of one of the hijackers. (Afterward, Miller would not remember the man's name or who his nephew was, but only one of the hijackers, Ziad Jarrah, was from Beirut.) Miller told the uncle that if he sent a DNA sample, the investigators would attempt to cross-reference it with human remains from the site. He never heard back from the man, but the call remains the only attempt of a relative to claim the remains of a hijacker.

• • •

The families of Flight 93 stood together at the White House. It had been just a week since they had visited the crash site, and here some of them were together again, being ushered into the East Room to meet the president, Laura Bush, and Secretary of Defense Rumsfeld. Gordie Felt found it "overwhelming" to be with other family members. Though they didn't know one another, they shared this terrible thing and were now going to talk about it with the president himself.

Grace Sherwood, the daughter of Jean Peterson and stepdaughter of Don Peterson, thought the president was just an awful public speaker. Bush kept repeating, "We're going to smoke them out of their holes," which didn't sit well with Sherwood because she didn't think that violence should be fought with more violence and more killing.

But then the president went into one of the side rooms and met with each family individually. Sherwood thought that was very nice of him, to spend ten minutes or so with each family. Gordie Felt found it amazing "to be holding the attention of the President of the United States and for him to talk with us about my brother."

When Ben Wainio, father of Honor Elizabeth Wainio, went in to meet Bush, Wainio held back tears and said, "Mister President, my daughter's name is Honor Elizabeth, and she honored her country by dying for it." His wife, Esther Heymann, who had loved Honor Elizabeth as her own daughter, was sobbing, and the president put his arms around her. "You just cry, mother," he said.

Lyz Glick, the wife of Jeremy Glick, found the experience mostly "bizarre." There she was, standing in the high-ceilinged room at the White House, holding her new baby and hearing the president mention her late husband's name. When she went into the other room and had a photo op with the president, she felt that meeting with all of those families was a very difficult thing for him to do. And then the White House staff served them cookies, which seemed bizarre in itself.

As she walked out at the close of the event, White House staffers lined the walls of the corridor holding little American flags, and they were crying. They thanked the families because the flight could have hit the White House, and here they were, seeing young women with babies who were now widows because their husbands had died instead of them. Glick thought it was beautiful that people were so caring. But it was still difficult being in that public place and not knowing what to say because you didn't want the staffers to feel bad.

• • •

The debate over who the "real" heroes on board Flight 93 were was becoming a real bone of contention. This debate, which had begun with John Murtha's positing one heroic individual, had made it to the House of Representatives in Washington, D.C. Just nine days after the flight, three bills were introduced proposing that Congress award the Congressional Gold Medal—the highest honor Congress can grant a civilian—posthumously to various people on board the plane. The problem was that the bills didn't agree on exactly who really deserved the medal.

A bill that singled out just one passenger, Jeremy Glick, was proposed by the representative from Glick's New Jersey district. It went nowhere in Congress. Next was a bill to award the Gold Medal to all four men thought to be "true" heroes—Glick, Todd Beamer, Tom Burnett, and Mark Bingham—and any other passengers and crew who could be verified by the U.S. attorney general as having aided in the effort to resist the hijackers. The bill's main sponsor, Representative Peter King of New York, advocated an "objective standard" of heroism for the medal's recipients. Passengers and crew who did not meet that standard would be recognized not with gold medals, but with gold coins.

This attitude angered many relatives of the passengers and crew. "Honor everybody or nobody," said Christine Fraser, whose sister Colleen was on Flight 93. President Bush himself apparently felt the same. On the day he hosted Flight 93 families at the White House, several families heard the president say, "They were all heroes." Senator Arlen Specter of Pennsylvania, in turn, thought everyone on the plane deserved a Gold Medal and drafted alternative legislation to that effect. His proposal died in the Senate. Subsequent bills proposed over the next decade would fare no better. They all foundered on the problem of gaining agreement on who exactly were the true heroes of the revolt. Glick, Beamer, Burnett, and Bingham were known to have announced their intentions over onboard phones. But what about those who might have been on the front line but didn't call anybody? The blunt truth was that no one will ever know precisely who fought on board Flight 93 in those last terrible moments.

What exactly defines a hero, anyway? The Pittsburgh-based Carnegie Hero Fund Commission uses the classical definition: "Someone who voluntarily leaves a point of safety to assume life risk to save or attempt to save the life of another." By this definition, even those who perform acts of great bravery don't necessarily deserve to be called heroes.

For example, U.S. Airways captain Chesley Sullenberger was widely hailed as a hero for safely landing his disabled airliner in the Hudson River in 2009. But after Sullenberger and his wife actually looked the word up in the dictionary, they decided that he didn't fit the definition. If a hero is someone who puts himself at risk in order to save another, said Sullenberger, "that didn't quite fit my situation, which was thrust upon me suddenly. Certainly, my crew and I were up to the task. But I'm not sure it quite crosses the threshold of heroism. I think the idea of a hero is important. But sometimes in our culture we overuse the word, and by overusing it we diminish it."

The Carnegie Hero Fund Commission did not award hero status to anyone on board Flight 93.

50   In the wake of September 11, the word "hero" could be employed very freely. One FBI agent who worked at the crash site asked whether "a gray-haired, sixty-five-year-old grandmother was any less a hero because she didn't charge the cockpit." At the Pentagon Memorial on its opening day, I heard a man speaking to a crowd about the Pentagon employees who had been killed in the attack. "Those people were heroes," he said. "They didn't know it, but they were heroes."

But by that standard, almost any unexpected death counts as heroism. In reality, the Pentagon victims were mostly office workers toiling away at routine bureaucratic tasks when fire and steel came crashing down on them. By what standard can such a death be called heroic?

The fact remained that the media had awarded de facto hero status to Jeremy Glick, Todd Beamer, Tom Burnett, and Mark Bingham while leaving the other passengers in shadow. This basic inequity subtly divided the families. Ultimately, to move ahead with memorial plans, the families came to a tacit agreement: publicly, everyone on the plane would be designated a hero. Failure to so agree would have torn the families of Flight 93 apart. Still, the "polite fiction," as some called it, never sat well with those family members who thought that their loved ones were the only "true" heroes. "I think it's a beautiful story that forty people rose as one but that's not the real story," said Alice Hoagland, whose son, Mark Bingham, was one of the few who were almost certain to have stormed the cockpit. Opinions like hers would quietly divide the families for years to come.

· · ·

Politicians and families might disagree about who the "real" heroes were, but the American people did not make such finicky distinctions. By this time, the belief that the passengers and crew had *willingly sacrificed themselves* for their country had swelled to the status of an American myth—this, despite the lack of any firm evidence from phone calls or the cockpit voice recorder to support the claim of self-sacrifice. Although their bravery is beyond dispute, what actually motivated the passengers and crew to take on the hijackers is anything but clear. Were they making a desperate attempt to land the plane and save their own lives? Or were they consciously sacrificing their lives "to save others on the ground," as President Bush had declared on national television?

The answer to that question will never be known. But to accept the latter explanation as fact is to enter the realm of mythology— though not in the popular sense of that word, which implies an untruth. A modern myth, by a better definition, is a compelling story that may or may not be factually true but that provokes a powerful response by using vivid, evocative symbols. By this definition, a myth is a way to cope with times of great upheaval, and in the national trauma that followed 9/11, the mythology of sacrifice for the nation was psychologically necessary for Americans to believe in. In any case, it would be quoted *as fact* in almost every political speech about Flight 93 from then on.

Not every family member is convinced of this mythology. Dale Nacke, the brother of Louis Nacke of the Superman tattoo, takes a more hardheaded view of his brother's motives in his likely participation in the passenger revolt: "They were just people, people who came together and did the extraordinary. People who gave their lives to save, not necessarily others, because I think their motivations were very self-serving and why wouldn't they be? Do you really think that they were concerned about the Capitol? I highly doubt it. I'm sure they were trying to save their own lives, and that is the most powerful motivator imaginable. That, to me, is much more powerful than the touting of them as, 'Well, they knew the plane was going to hit the Capitol.' They didn't have a freaking idea where that plane was going. They came together as one to save themselves, and that is very powerful and very moving. And I am very proud of my brother for being part of it, as I am proud of everybody on that plane."

Nor do all family members cling to the belief that their loved ones had *any* role in the passenger revolt. "I don't think Mom and Don were up there fighting with the hijackers," said Grace Sherwood, daughter of Jean Peterson and stepdaughter of Don Peterson, both of whom died on the flight. "They were sitting in the back, holding each other and praying. In hindsight, I'm glad they were together because the thought of them being alone without anybody else. . . .

I don't want to dwell on those last twenty minutes. I'd like to think about what they did in their lives."

• • •

"Every era, every culture deals with grief and mourning and loss," says contemporary artist Dario Robleto, who has been called a "sculptor of memory." "Creativity [is] the response to the loss. . . . The loss [insists] on some sort of aesthetic. Writing a poem. Making an object. Something."

Robleto writes, "These objects ask very human moral questions: What right do we have to forget? What do we owe to each other's memories?"

Creative acts are a specific response to grieving for a personality type that psychologist Susan Berger labels the "memorialist." In *The Five Ways We Grieve*, Berger explains that the memorialist's main way of honoring and remembering a loved one is by visible or tangible memorials, such as rituals and artifacts. Through these, the memorialist maintains a living connection with the loved one. Paintings, songs, books inspired by the loved one, rituals performed yearly, memory gardens, and, of course, stone-and-mortar memorials are among memorialists' typical creations.

A prime example of a memorialist was Derrill Bodley, the father of Deora Bodley, a junior at Santa Clara University who had died in the crash. Bodley had always been extraordinarily close to his daughter, by all accounts an outstanding young woman with a lifelong interest in world peace. She volunteered for community literacy and was studying to be a child psychologist. She and her father talked by phone almost every day, and he would often travel from his home in Stockton to Santa Clara for walks in the gardens together. Deora was absolutely central to his life, and her death was devastating.

Music turned out to be at least a partial salvation for Bodley, a professor of music. A day or two after Deora's death, he was sitting at the piano and felt that he heard Deora saying very clearly, *I'm all right, Dad. Just do the right thing.* And music began to just flow through him. The result was "Steps to Peace," a beautiful composition that was recorded by jazz musician Dave Brubeck. "It's like she wrote it for me," said Bodley.

But creative memorials are no cure-all. Berger found that memorialists can experience protracted grieving periods and can feel isolated in their grief, as if no one has experienced what they have. The fact that "Steps to Peace" was recorded by a leading jazz musician helped Bodley break out of his isolated grief, but it did not bring closure or anything like closure to this intensely grieving father. Those first holidays take a special toll on survivors, and on the Christmas following the crash, Bodley wound up in the hospital, thinking he was having a heart attack. It turned out he was simply suffering from extreme stress.

Berger found that the more closely memorialists identify with other survivors—as did the Flight 93 families, who banded together to create a national memorial—the more they can gain some measure of comfort from knowing they are not alone. Whether they found comfort or not, however, many family members and Shanksville residents believed that remembering the forty was a moral imperative that would demand years of intense commitment.

As Dario Robleto would put it: What right did they have to forget? What did they owe to the memories of forty people?

53

4

IF MEMORIES

COULD HEAL

It was a bitterly cold December afternoon three months after 9/11, with no snow on the ground, when Ed Linenthal toured the crash site. A scholar of religion, he had spent his career studying and writing about memory and the making of memorials at various sites, including American battlefields from Lexington and Concord to Pearl Harbor, the Enola Gay exhibit at the Smithsonian Institution, and the Holocaust Museum in Washington, D.C.

After the Oklahoma City bombing, he moved to that city to document the bomb's aftermath and the long, painful journey of planning and building a memorial. It was Linenthal's intimate knowledge of the Oklahoma City experience that prompted the NPS to bring him to Shanksville for a town meeting, intended primarily to help local people take the first small steps toward planning a memorial and to explore what that would mean for Somerset County.

Linenthal's book about Oklahoma City, *The Unfinished Bombing*, had been published just a few weeks before 9/11. Linenthal was trying to keep himself from being excited about the fact that so many people saw it as relevant to 9/11, because if he got excited, what did that say about him? What made the situation even more chilling was that in the conclusion of the book he had foreseen another terrorist attack of greater magnitude than Oklahoma City, positing that the Murrah Federal Building bombing might be the first in a crescendo of terrorist attacks.

As Linenthal walked through the debris field, he was struck by the disconnect between the quiet beauty of the place and the horror of what had happened there. Sometimes we expect horrific events to have occurred at sites that are ugly, but Linenthal knew that that often isn't the case. Walking in the grove of hemlocks where all the debris from the plane had been flung by the blast, Linenthal found it an incredibly "eloquent" place, quiet and compelling, with the wind blowing through the trees. He immediately had a sense that this was sacred ground. The television images of a smoking hole hadn't given him an inkling of what it was like to stand here, and he was simply stunned by the power of it. 55

The grove threw him back in time to a trip to Poland that he had taken when he was writing his book on the making of the United States Holocaust Memorial Museum. There, he had walked near the mass graves at Chelmno, where, in 1941, almost half a million Jews were murdered in gas vans and their remains burned. To this day, especially when it rains, the material evidence of their lives seeps slowly to the surface. *Land always remembers*, thought Linenthal.

Linenthal's research had taught him that the corrosive, toxic impact of horrific events is enduring. He was skeptical that healthy communities could reemerge atop piles of dead bodies—which, if he was right, spelled dark days ahead for Shanksville.

He also wondered about the tremendous acceleration of people's desire to memorialize, and about how immediately Americans were beginning to respond to mass tragedies in places such as Oklahoma City and, now, Shanksville. There seemed to be a rush to construct memorials as a gesture of civic renewal. Building something was supposed to make sense out of the horror of the events, he thought; it was an illusory way of saying, "It's over. We've memorialized it. Now we can put it away. We can put it on the memorial bookshelf and move on to something else."

. . .

Is there, in fact, a rush to construct memorials in America? Notably, during just one presidency, George W. Bush dedicated a slew of major memorials: the National World War II Memorial, the Air Force Memorial, the National D-Day Memorial, the Victims of

Communism Memorial, the Valor in the Pacific Memorial (which includes the memorial to the attack on Pearl Harbor), and, of course, the 9/11 Pentagon Memorial.

New memorials keep rolling out, many of which attest to the dark tide of violence in this country, as evidenced by the memorials to school shootings such as those that occurred at Columbine High School and Virginia Tech. At least five hundred recorded memorials, large and small, would eventually be dedicated to 9/11 alone.

In contrast to historic *monuments* to memory—statues of soldiers in the public square, stone generals on horseback on a Civil War battlefield, obelisks or other freestanding carved blocks of stone—contemporary memorials are mostly *landscape* memorials. They are part of their sites, and they can be walked through and, in some cases, sat on or climbed on. Increasingly, the memorial is located on the spot where the terrible event took place—the site of the Pentagon 9/11 disaster, for example. It is unthinkable to locate such memorials anywhere other than in the landscapes that give them meaning.

"Why do we make memorials in America today—and why do we make so many of them?" Erika Doss asks in *Memorial Mania*. "Just in the past few decades, thousands of new memorials to executed witches, enslaved Africans, victims of terrorism, victims of lynching, dead astronauts, aborted fetuses, and murdered teenagers have materialized in the American landscape." The proliferation of such memorials testifies, says Doss, to "an obsession with issues of memory and history and an urgent desire to express and claim those issues in visibly public contexts. Today's growing numbers of memorials represent *heightened anxieties* about who and what should be remembered in America."

Does building a memorial, then, ensure that an event will be remembered? Not necessarily. "The inevitability of forgetting is already implicit in these memorials," write Robert Hariman and John Louis Lucaites in their essay "Vernacular Memorials and Civic Decline." "Why else do we have to be told to remember?"

On the cold December evening of the town meeting in Shanksville, however, no one could even imagine forgetting what had happened at the strip mine outside the village. The meeting was held at Shanksville-Stonycreek High School, at the edge of town. It was a milestone that would put the NPS squarely in charge of the memorial planning process from then on.

The auditorium was full. The meeting began with an invitation for local people to come to the microphone, and themes emerged that would carry forward over the coming years. The NPS had brought in speakers from Oklahoma City, people who were familiar with the making of a memorial to a mass tragedy, simply to talk about their experiences—what worked, what didn't. Oklahoma City's process of creating a memorial would soon become the model for Shanksville, although that was not the intent early on.

Joanne Hanley, superintendent of the national parks of western Pennsylvania, stressed that the meeting would be the first of many steps in "a long, deliberate and intentional process of memorialization and remembrance." At this time, no decisions would be made on what the memorial would look like or where it would be located.

Some locals, however, already knew what they wanted the memorial to look like. Janet Coughenour rose to the microphone and recalled the night she had seen the fifteen-thousand-pound flag displayed at Jennerstown Speedway. "It was raining that evening," she said, "and I just thought, it looks like our nation's tears are on that flag. And I thought a huge flag should be covering the crash site. Not that flag in particular, but perhaps a flag made of durable material like ceramic tile. And in the stars, the victims' names could be engraved just like the stars in the Hollywood Walk of Fame. And that way that flag could be seen from far and wide, even from the air. We can't change the tragic events of September 11, but perhaps as Americans we can show the world what true patriotism is all about."

Robert Leverknight from nearby Lambertsville rose to speak. He agreed that the memorial should be built, but his long-range concern was that commercialism could turn this sweet rural area into another Gettysburg or Valley Forge, overrun with fast-food joints, chain motels, and outlet stores. "I never in my life thought of myself as a 'not-in-my-backyard' kind of person," Leverknight said. "My personal feeling, though, is I don't want a McDonald's across the street from me. What kind of protection is going to be put in place against rampant commercial development?"

It was the right question, but it was being asked in the wrong place. In conservative Somerset County, locals were dead set against zoning regulations or any other controls on what an owner could do with his land. Leverknight's question would go unanswered.

FIG. 5 "Father Al" Mascherino. Photo: *Johnstown Tribune-Democrat* (John Rucosky).

Although the design of a final, built memorial was premature, several moveable and wearable memorials debuted that night. A state representative in Pennsylvania had initiated the idea of Hearts of Steel bracelets, modeled on the POW bracelets from the Vietnam War. Each bracelet read, "We remember 9-11-01." Beneath that, some added "United we stand" and others "Let's roll." Companies in western Pennsylvania donated the steel and the fabrication. The proceeds from the bracelets' sale would all go toward the memorial. Eventually, one hundred thousand would be sold.

• • •

Then Phil Thompson was introduced, invited from Oklahoma City to share that city's experience of planning a memorial. He had served on the project's family services committee. Thompson's mother had been buried in the collapse of the Murrah Federal Building. Her remains were not recovered until forty-two days after the bombing, and then only part of them. So Thompson knew a lot about grief and working with families who were convulsed by grief.

"Thank you for inviting me to be here tonight," said Thompson, "though I deeply regret having to be here. I shouldn't have to tell you what my story's about, nor should I even have to have a story. But unfortunately, all of us have been thrown together here to try to do something together."

Thompson talked about how a good outcome was achieved in Oklahoma City. It was process, process, process, he said. It was hard to reach a consensus on tough, controversial issues, but consensus was essential. It wasn't going to be quick or painless. The memorial-planning process is uncomfortable, he said, because you are dealing with family members who are in such great pain, and you don't know how to communicate with them. And you can't expect their pain, or your own, to go away anytime soon.

"I've heard the word 'closure' used," said Thompson. "In the beginning we used the word quite a bit. 'Closure. Can't wait till we have closure.' I will tell you that closure does not exist. It's a journey and we go from plateau to plateau. But this memorial process was one we used to help people heal.

"The one thing about a memorial is that there's a great day of the dedication. That day I walked out on the memorial site and, for the first time in a long, long time, I was able to smile at the thought of my mother. Not this gut-wrenching pain."

The reward was there, said Thompson—if not an end to suffering, at least an abatement of it. Based on the Oklahoma City experience, the journey to a memorial could be a *healing journey*.

■ ■ ■

At the same time that the town meeting was coming together, a white-haired Catholic priest was combing the back roads of Somerset County, searching for a venue for his own personal memorial.

Many local people viewed the passenger revolt through the lens of their faith. "God bless Flight 93" was a common sentiment written on mementos at the straw-bale altar near the crash site. No local resident, however, acted on the faith connection so wholeheartedly or carried it to such lengths as did "Father Al" Mascherino.

He was not your average country priest. In his late fifties, he was currently unassigned to any parish because of his history of bipolar disorder. His elevated energy levels and mood swings left him unfit for the stresses of parish life. His choice of treatment for the disorder, hypnotherapy, was also unorthodox.

Among the rumors that circulated in the weeks after the crash, there was one—never confirmed—that the Flight 93 passengers prayed together before launching the revolt. (Todd Beamer did recite the Lord's Prayer and part of the 23rd Psalm via cell phone with the GTE-Verizon operator, but there was no recorded evidence of a group prayer.) Father Al, however, didn't need any evidence. He was convinced that the passengers "prayed together, [asking] God for guidance and direction and courage and strength, and the faith of Americans," before taking action. Out of that certitude came the conviction that the most appropriate memorial to Flight 93 would be a *memorial of faith*.

The government, he knew, would never build such a memorial—you couldn't even say a prayer without a permit nowadays. And he heard via the county commissioners that the national memorial would take five to ten years to build. So Father Al decided that he would build the memorial to God and the heroes himself.

He had no idea what form the memorial would take, but began by looking around at abandoned churches in the region. As luck would have it, he found one just outside Shanksville on Stutzmantown Road. It was a former Lutheran church, surrounded by cornfields, just three miles from the crash site. An old country cemetery was across the road. The building had been used as a seed warehouse for years and now was practically falling down, with mice nesting in the walls. It was for sale.

The problem was that, as an unassigned priest, Father Al was not receiving a salary and only had $300 in the bank. But he had long collected antiques and other memorabilia, and he sold some antique Christmas ornaments to come up with the small down payment. Around Christmas he had a dream—a very vivid dream—about how the chapel was going to be decorated, what he was going to put where, and what it would all look like. On Christmas Day he went down to his mother's basement and sketched what he had seen in the dream—sketched like a man possessed for twenty-four hours straight.

As soon as he closed on the property on January 9, 2002, Father Al drove right out there and said a prayer of thanksgiving. He knelt down and cried, because this was something so immense that he couldn't comprehend it. He knew he was being swept along by something that had energy of its own. Then he picked up his tools and started working. He planned to chip away at the restoration via sweat equity—his own sweat—for as long as it took. So he started working on that bitter-cold January day with no heat in the building. He worked until his toes got so numb he could barely walk.

· · ·

On the other side of the world, a United Nations plane touched down at a military airport outside Kabul, Afghanistan. On board were four Americans who had lost family members at various September 11 sites. One of them was Derrill Bodley, whose beloved daughter Deora was on Flight 93.

Not all the Flight 93 families favored a full-scale military response to the terrorist attacks, but Bodley viewed such a response with ab- solute horror. "Derrill was just horrified that his daughter's death, this peace-loving child's death, would be used by the administration as an excuse to go cause other harm and devastation and death," said his wife, Nancy. Estimates of Afghan civilian casualties already numbered in the thousands. So here he was in Afghanistan, in hopes of understanding what was really going on.

The trip took place under the auspices of September Eleventh Families for Peaceful Tomorrows, a group of family members opposed to the military response. Of course, their message went against the American grain. It could even be seen as unpatriotic, undermining the effort to oust the Taliban and find the Al-Qaeda hideouts.

It was a trip Bodley almost didn't make. He, like most family members of the 9/11 victims, was afraid to fly anywhere after the attacks, much less to the most dangerous country in central Asia. And he had recently been in the hospital suffering stress-related symptoms. Three others who had signed up had already dropped out. But, in the end, a woman who lost her brother in the Twin Towers convinced Bodley to go. So here he was, bumping along the road into the city as their van maneuvered around bomb craters and was stopped every few miles by soldiers brandishing Kalashnikovs. Nearing Kabul, they passed a bombed-out mosque that evoked memories of the wreckage of the World Trade Center.

Over the next four days, Bodley would meet with civilians whose lives had been gutted by the war, from land-mine victims to children injured by cluster bombs. He cried with one father, with whom he shared a photo of Deora. The father had lost his five-year-old daughter to a U.S. bomb that landed near their apartment building while the little girl was playing. Seeing the grief of this and other Afghan families helped put Bodley's own grief in perspective.
Bodley returned to the United States committed to working for peace in the face of the Bush administration's determination to apply a

military solution. His first act was to donate much of the money he received from a United Airlines settlement to relief projects in Afghanistan, to which he was already planning to return. But although Bodley's work for peace may have given him a sense of direction in the midst of his own grief, neither his nor Peaceful Tomorrows' efforts would make the least dent in the war in Afghanistan, which would outlast Bush's two terms as president and become the longest war in American history.

. . .

Back at the crash site, the tide of visitors continued to swell. Even the brutal Somerset County winters had not put a stop to them, as county leaders had thought it might. But without signage of any kind, the site was difficult to find and even more difficult to decipher once you got there. Some visitors assumed that a pile of scrap metal at the top of the hill was the remains of the plane. (The crater had been backfilled, so there was no clue as to where the plane actually hit.)

Local curator Barbara Black went to the temporary memorial every day to collect mementos people had left. She saw visitors coming, with no one there to meet them. She discussed the problem with Donna Glessner, who worried that no one was at the site to tell visitors the real story or point to where the plane went down.

"Barbara, we just can't have people coming to our community and not be taken care of," said Glessner. "They leave and they've had no contact with anyone here. This isn't right." So Glessner, a small, energetic woman, stood up in church the next Sunday and said, "Would anyone volunteer to help me take shifts out at the memorial just to talk to people, to have a human presence there?"

The volunteers called themselves the ambassadors and started in January 2002—a bitter-cold month in Shanksville to venture outdoors for any reason. "At first, it wasn't the story of what happened on the plane because that information was just being released in increments," Glessner said. "We mainly oriented people to the site and gave information about where they could go for gas or directions to the highways."

Sometimes the ambassadors' concern for visitors went beyond just giving directions. One day, Esther Heymann, stepmother of Honor Elizabeth Wainio, stood in a snowstorm, looking out over the empty field. She had driven up from her home near Baltimore,

FIG. 6 Flight 93 Ambassador Kathie Shaffer speaks to visitors at the temporary memorial. Photo: Chuck Wagner.

and she couldn't stop crying. Like many family members, she felt drawn to this wounded site, where the wounded family members felt closest to those they had lost. But January was no time to be standing out in the open anywhere around Shanksville.

Heymann was not entirely alone at the crash site. A volunteer ambassador, sheltered from the storm in his car, watched over her, and from time to time he ventured out to ask if she was all right. Finally, he invited her home for some warm soup and to wait for the storm to abate.

Such empathy for family members was common in Shanksville. Shirley Hillegass, who lived three miles from the crash site and saw Heymann crying during another visit, told Heymann her own story of losing her daughter in a car accident. Over time, the two mothers grew close. They talked about their daughters—vivacious young career women who were alike in many ways.

Among the tributes at the temporary memorial were forty painted angels on sticks. The angel inscribed with Honor Elizabeth's name bore a photo of her wearing jeans and a short-sleeved shirt. Heymann worried about her stepdaughter's exposure to Shanksville's brutal winters. "She's not dressed for snow, and I feel so impotent," Heymann said. "I wish I could keep her safe." In response, Hillegass checked on the photo when Heymann was not present.

Some ambassadors undertook their volunteerism with almost religious devotion. Chuck Wagner said that his life priorities were "my family, my church, Flight 93." Eventually, their over-the-top devotion would begin to have side effects. Some ambassadors' children resented the long hours that their parents spent at the crash site. Even Glessner admitted that her own kids, while proud of her work at the memorial, "see it as something that has taken me away from the family."

Still, the visitors kept coming in the thousands each month. The ambassadors recorded their numbers on handheld clickers and wrote them in a logbook—numbers that could not and should not be ignored. Some had traveled a long way expressly to be there, while for others it was a spontaneous detour off the turnpike.

But the crash site was not a place to visit lightly. "This ain't Disneyland" was how visitor Jim Gaydos put it. He had driven ten hours from Merrillville, Indiana, to visit the memorial. He was wearing a Klingon cap, which he treasured for its reference to a mythic race from *Star Trek* who lived by a code of honor. At the site, he took his cap from his head and respectfully dropped it on the ever-growing 65 temporary memorial.

Before heading back to Indiana, Gaydos picked up a few Shanksville rocks by which to remember the experience. "I didn't expect it to be this deep," he said.

The ambassadors handed out lots of Kleenexes. Donna Glessner got used to sights such as big, grizzled bikers in leather garb who had tears running down their faces from behind their dark glasses.

Shanksville residents had to replace the overloaded straw-bale altar that overlooked the crash site with a thirty-foot chain-link fence on which visitors could hang tributes. It looked much like the fence at the bombing site in Oklahoma City, which had been appropriated for exactly the same purpose. The similarity was no accident, since the Oklahoma City commemorative process served as the model for most of what was to unfold in Shanksville. Soon the entire fence was filled with messages, scrawled on everything from whitewashed boards to caps to teddy bears to paper plates. Every day at the site became reminiscent of Mexico's Day of the Dead (without the offerings of food and drink, of course).

After arriving, many visitors felt compelled to leave something—anything—as a tribute, objects they'd often find by digging around in their cars. A family from Louisiana with three teenage daughters first walked around like tourists, snapping pictures, then ended up studying the tributes and messages on the chain-link fence. The girls disappeared into the parking area and soon reappeared with a single Adidas shoe. Outside and inside the shoe they wrote, "I am Amelia and I am proud to be an America [sic]," "You will always be in my heart," and "United We Stand, Land of the Free, Home of the Brave." They hadn't planned to leave the shoe or anything else, but once there it seemed that they just had to leave some tribute—exactly why, they couldn't say.

Most of the messages left at the memorial, like those written by the girls from Louisiana, were addressed to an understood "you"—namely, the passengers and crew. "Thank you for protecting our country." "You made me believe in heroes." "I told my daughter this is sacred ground now, ground made sacred by heroic sacrifice. God bless you!" "We will not forget you." These visitors seemingly experienced this humble, handmade memorial as a portal through which the living could raise their voices to the dead—as if the passengers and crew were in some sense present, could be felt and sensed *here*, in this place.

Rhoda Schuler, a theology student from Minnesota who visited the temporary memorial in 2003, thought she knew what was behind these mass visits and mass tributes: American civil religion. This theory, conceived by sociologist Robert Bellah in the late 1970s, recognizes a nonsectarian religious structure in Americans' beliefs about their country. According to civil religion, America is "God's country," subject to divine favor, guidance, protection, and judgment. Civil religion in America, Bellah thought, was born and tested in two times of trial, the Revolution and the Civil War.

Schuler believed that the events of September 11 ushered in a new time of trial, one in which the American people sought answers to questions regarding the source of evil, the deaths of the innocent, and God's role in such events. She viewed acts of pilgrimage as embodying these questions.

Schuler made her own pilgrimage to Shanksville to test her interpretation. She pored over the messages left at the temporary memorial, observing and interviewing visitors and volunteer ambassadors. Again and again, she found the themes of civil religion in people's reactions to the crash. Of these themes, the most important was the almost universal reference to the crash site as "sacred ground."

The ambassadors reported that virtually all of the visitors acted as if they were in church, and they spoke of their ambassadorial duty as a "sacred" trust. Many visitors seemed, in fact, to be enacting a traditional religious pilgrimage—something "told them" to come. Finally, said Schuler, the forty heroes provided "a glimpse, if only through a glass darkly, of an answer to that ultimate question: Why did this happen to the nation?"

Why, indeed, had this happened to America? History and geopolitics would surely provide clues, but historically, as Ed Linenthal would point out, Americans haven't liked to dwell on complex issues such as U.S. involvement in the Middle East, preferring a simpler, more heroic narrative. In the collective trauma that followed 9/11, American heroes were more needed than ever, and the forty passengers and crew emerged as the *necessary heroes* of a new American mythology.

· · ·

By the February after the crash, the arduous process of identifying the remains had been completed. Each victim had been positively identified. But Miller realized that he had one further major duty to perform. As the remains were returned to the families, he said, "some people were going to look inside the caskets and I wanted them to know it would be shocking." In some cases the contents of the casket would be nothing more than a finger.

He had to explain to the families what they would or would not be receiving of their loved ones. The problem was that there was no money available to bring the families together. Just when Miller was at his wits' end, a woman from the Allegheny County United Way called and said that she had a large number of donations that were earmarked for the families of Flight 93.

Armed with this windfall, Miller arranged for a mass meeting of next of kin at a New Jersey hotel, against the advice of many people, including United Airlines, who did not think that the families would be able to handle the grim news he had to deliver. "Well, they're going to have to handle it," said Miller. "They need information." Miller and Arlene put together a PowerPoint presentation that explained the recovery protocol they'd followed. Miller didn't really think that many would come, but they did. Thirty-six of the forty families gathered—a total of eighty-eight people—in that New Jersey hotel suite to discuss the return of their loved ones, or what was left of them.

Miller had never actually stood in front of the assembled families of the victims. He had talked to most of them over the phone for the last five months and had met a number of them one-on-one at the crash site. Standing in front of those gathered faces to deliver the difficult news, however, was different, and Miller broke down.

He stood there in front of the families and cried for ten minutes. At one point some of the families actually began to applaud, because they understood that this wasn't just a job for Miller, that he had taken on their grief.

Soon after that meeting, the families received their loved ones' remains, even if these were only a tooth and a lock of hair. Male victims were returned in an eighteen-gauge onyx metal casket, and women in a similar pink casket. The caskets were paid for by the airline and, of course, were almost entirely empty; what was there was best not looked at. A few remains were cremated locally and returned in cherry-wood urns.

• • •

Now Miller, who had always been terrified of public speaking, was increasingly in demand as a speaker at gatherings of coroners, emergency rescue workers, and law enforcement officers from New Orleans to Vancouver. He received an honorary doctorate in social justice from Mount Aloysius College in 2002. But Miller didn't much enjoy travel, especially if it involved flying. Seeing the innate fragility of the destroyed jetliner had left its mark. "You see all that wire, and if one of them goes wrong—you're down," he said. "It's a frightening thought." Anyway, Miller wasn't sold on the idea that there should be any demand for his expertise. Asked how audiences responded to his speeches, Miller laughed. "I think they were surprised at what a rube I was."

At the Somerset Alliance Church on the six-month anniversary of the crash, Miller expressed a different take on the crash. Friends had convinced him "that this is the time and place to speak of the spiritual aspect of what happened out there." But first he wanted to make it clear that he had no special qualifications for the discussion or for what he had done since 9/11.

"I am a Christian," he told the church audience. "I'm not an exemplary Christian." For some reason, which remained unknown to him, he said, "God put me in charge of the site. This is not something I want to be remembered for. It was part of my journey." Raised in the Church of the Brethren, Miller would convert to Catholicism in the aftermath of the crash. "Nothing brings you closer to religion than death," he said.

"I don't care about fame and notoriety," Miller further declared. "I believe everything we do brings us to a final accounting of ourselves, and when that final accounting comes, I'm going to say, 'I am Wallace Miller and I'm a hick. I made a lot of mistakes, but I did the best I could with the resources we had.'"

• • •

Donna Glessner and the Flight 93 ambassadors thought of the temporary memorial as "the people's place." The people's offerings were clearly heartfelt, though the specifics varied astonishingly. Some of the mementos were thoughtfully crafted and composed. There was a carved granite memorial from a man in Guatemala and several handmade quilts. Others were rarities, such as a brick that an American soldier had brought back from a Taliban compound in Afghanistan. The vast majority of items people left, however, were 69 knickknacks and cheap manufactured goods—caps, flags, license plates, teddy bears.

"Imagine a school assignment," write scholars Robert Hariman and John Louis Lucaites, "where students are required to write a memorial essay using only five nouns." For Hariman and Lucaites, this would be comparable to the "same, limited iconography" that is repeated over and over at memorials such as the one in Shanksville. This small repertoire of cheap manufactured tributes, they contend, ensures maximum intelligibility at the cost of being unable to say much that is nuanced or distinctive. Of course, it is a testimony to the power of visual media that just a few images are sufficient to communicate powerful emotions and foster collective bonding.

Barbara Black, however, did not discriminate against tributes according to their provenance. She came by practically every day to collect items for storage. Everything, except live flowers, was carefully preserved and archived for display at the visitor center that was supposed to be built one day. When the tens of thousands of items overflowed the Somerset Historical Society, she started shipping the excess to a secure storage facility in Butler, Pennsylvania.

In the face of an avalanche of tributes, Black resisted deeming unique craft objects as more worth keeping than mass-produced knickknacks. "We are not making judgments as to what's valuable," she said. "That note written by a child, or a harmonica left on a rock, each has as much significance as a carefully composed poem or a beautifully drawn picture. We treat everything as if it were a treasured historical object."

■ ■ ■

The cockpit voice recording that had been unearthed just outside Shanksville was now at the center of a brouhaha among Flight 93 families across the country. They wanted the FBI to let them hear it. In California, Deena Burnett, whose husband, Tom Burnett, was one of the leaders of the revolt, said, "I lie awake at night wondering what he thought and what he felt. . . . I think that by hearing what happened in the last moment of his life perhaps that would provide a little bit more of a picture."

The FBI initially refused to release even an edited transcript of the voice recorder on the grounds that it was evidence in an air-crash investigation. But victims' rights groups supported the families' right to know. Then Burnett's congresswoman added pressure to the FBI, which finally acquiesced in an unprecedented departure from bureau procedure.

Not all family members felt that hearing the passengers' anguished final moments was such a good idea. Mitchell Zykofsky, whose stepfather, John Talignani, was on the flight, said, "I can't see how hearing how people were killed could help."

But one day in April, about seventy family members—representatives from all but a handful of the families—from all over the United States gathered in a Princeton, New Jersey, hotel to hear the tape. The FBI warned them that the recording was "violent and very distressing. Once the [cockpit voice recorder] is heard, it may be impossible to forget the sounds and images it evokes." Mental health personnel were on hand just in case.

Expectations ran high among the families. "I expect my husband's voice to be on [the tape]," Burnett said. She was not alone in that conviction. But when the tape began to roll, it was hard to tell what was said, much less who was speaking. The voices were muddled and occasionally drowned out by the sound of wind rushing outside the cockpit as the plane traveled at 575 miles per hour at low altitude. You couldn't discern individuals even when they were yelling at the top of their lungs.

Sandy Dahl, however, was convinced she heard the terrorists talking to her husband, Jason. As she sat next to Melody Homer, the wife of the copilot, they held hands and attempted to identify voices they recognized. Dahl became convinced that "Jason actually stayed in the cockpit alone with the hijacker-pilot, injured but not dead, for quite a long time." Appearing later on *Good Morning America*, she insisted that "they fussed at him to stay down. . . . They fussed at him for a good six to ten minutes to 'stop touching that.'" Was Jason Dahl trying to put the plane on autopilot before he lost consciousness? She was sure he was.

At one point in the thirty-minute tape, the families heard a woman crying "Oh God, oh God" and pleading for her life. Later came the sound of someone gurgling and groaning. Still, for the families, hearing the passengers breaking into the cockpit confirmed that they were heroes.

FBI agents and New Jersey state troopers escorted family members to their cars at the end of the session. But Alice Hoagland, mother of passenger Mark Bingham, chose to speak to the press; together with Deena Burnett, Hoagland had spearheaded the effort to allow families to hear the tape. After Lisa Beamer, Hoagland was to become the most televised of the Flight 93 family members. Her outgoing personality and her eloquence in talking about the tragedy, often with an expression resembling a smile, made her play very well on the television screen. Today she wasn't smiling—her face was contorted with grief. But although the experience had been "excruciating," she told reporters she was glad she had listened to the tape, adding, "I wish there was a video."

• • •

One of the transformative effects of Flight 93 on Shanksville was that it cracked open this sleepy hollow to the world. Together with tens of thousands of ordinary Americans who flocked to the temporary memorial, the nation's movers and shakers began to find their way to the village.

In May 2002, the Shanksville High School graduation ceremony received the most unlikely of visitors: Rudolph Giuliani, the mayor of New York City. Gina Walker, the president of the Shanksville senior class, had had the chutzpah to write to Giuliani, inviting him to speak at the graduation of their minuscule high school senior class. Meagen Beisterling, who helped with the letter, thought that "never in a million years" would Giuliani accept the invitation. Yet here he was.

In his speech, Giuliani admitted that it was a bit of a culture shock to come from America's largest city to a village with a graduating class of thirty-six. But, the mayor said, Shanksville and New York were now inextricably bound together in the war against terrorism.

"Do not be afraid," he told the students. "Be ready for the worst, but be brave. Those who died on September 11 did not die for us to live afraid."

Despite his talk of bravery, Giuliani took no chances on his visit. After flying into Johnstown, he traveled to Shanksville by motorcade, accompanied by his own security force and twelve state troopers. A private security firm also worked at the event, while a state police helicopter circled the school.

After his talk Giuliani shook hands with each of the students as they received their diplomas, and he posed for photographs with them. "This is a happy day and that's a sad thing," Meagan Beisterling reflected. "Our entire senior year has been about Flight 93; we've had about a million special services. Shanksville is a red, white, and blue town. . . . Nobody will ever be able to actually forget what happened here."

• • •

In Washington, D.C., the wheels were turning to authorize a permanent memorial on the crash site. In March 2002, Congressman John Murtha introduced a bill in the House of Representatives that would establish a national memorial administered by the NPS. In April, Senator Arlen Specter of Pennsylvania introduced a similar bill in the Senate. In September, these bills passed both houses of Congress, and President Bush signed the Flight 93 National Memorial Act, authorizing the NPS to develop a permanent memorial. It included appropriations for first steps—for the NPS to purchase the first parcels of land, rent a local office, train the ambassadors, and set up a process that would lead to a memorial design.

Back in Shanksville, Father Al wasn't waiting for the lumbering progress of the federal government to create a memorial to his heroes. He continued to sell his personal antiques, and every time he had $50 in hand, he would go to the local 84 Lumber store and purchase lumber and nails for the restoration of the defunct church out on Stutzmantown Road. He came by so often that employees at 84 Lumber started asking questions, and Father Al was only too happy to talk. Soon Maggie Hardy Magerko, the owner of the company, got wind of the project, and she immediately chipped in $23,000 in supplies. News of the project spread by word of mouth, and volunteers started coming by to pitch in. Still, progress was slow.

Now a bigger problem was looming: Father Al's commitment to the chapel had run afoul of Bishop Joseph Adamec of the Altoona-Johnstown Diocese. To begin with, Roman Catholic priests weren't supposed to go around founding churches. But it went deeper than that. Bishop Adamec had long looked askance at Father Al, suspecting that his bipolar disorder and his stubborn insistence that

FIG. 8   Father Al's Flight 93 Memorial Chapel on Stutzmantown Road. Photo: J. Stephen Conn.

hypnotherapy would cure it left him unfit to be a priest. Now Father Al's over-the-top involvement in the chapel was further indication of his imbalance. Finally, Bishop Adamec gave him an ultimatum: "Either you go or the chapel goes."

That August, Hardy Magerko visited the church and saw how truly desperate the condition of the place was. She told Father Al that the chapel needed to be in shape for the first anniversary of the crash and put a small army of professional builders at Father Al's disposal. They worked around the clock for ten days, using the sketches he had drawn on Christmas as blueprints. At 4:00 P.M. on September 10, 2002, the artist applying gold-leaf paint to the trim in the sanctuary put his brush down and the work was complete. The ultimate cost of the restoration, paid for by Hardy Magerko, was estimated at $150,000. The result was a stunning demonstration of the speed at which private initiative could get things done, as compared to the slow march of government action (or inaction) at the crash site three miles away.

The finished chapel reflected Father Al's somewhat flamboyant taste in decoration, with no fewer than five chandeliers. The altar was done in a Federalist style representing the Capitol, which was saved by the passenger revolt, and topped by a large gold eagle sculpture. A small meditation room off to the side contained framed pictures of the forty victims, each lit by a red-glass votive candle. In front of the church was a new forty-foot bell tower with a "thunder bell," whose ring, it was said, could be heard at the crash site three miles away.

Through the generosity of a single benefactor, the quixotic vision of one man had been realized. And it was, above all, an *individual* vision. There had been no committee to bring on board, no wrenching effort to reach a consensus. "The chapel is my expression of the way *I* want to honor and memorialize the heroes of Flight 93," said Father Al. "It was my compulsion to honor them in some way."

One year into the post-9/11 era, then, the wheels had just started to creak toward building a permanent national memorial at the crash site. But out on Stutzmantown Road, between the cornfields and the country cemetery, the first permanent memorial to Flight 93 was already in place.

• • •

One day Wally Miller received a call from the White House. As a first responder, he was invited to a concert at the Kennedy Center for the Performing Arts in Washington, D.C., that September, and as a special honor the White House invited him to sit in the box with the president.

"Wow!" said Miller. "I've got to tell my wife—we're going meet the President."

"No—not your wife. Just you," said the White House staffer. "This is just for first responders. She can sit down below, but we want you to sit up in the President's box."

"My wife handled every remain that came out of there," said Miller. "I'm not coming if she can't come."

"Rudy Giuliani's girlfriend's not going to be in the box either," countered the staffer.

"Well, it's important what you just said," Miller replied. "It's his girlfriend. This is my wife. I'm not coming without her." And that was the end of it. Miller didn't know who went to the concert in Washington, but he didn't go.

• • •

On the first anniversary of the crash, a crowd five hundred strong— Flight 93 family and friends from all over the country, together with locals—gathered at the crash site. There was to be a ceremony of remembrance, a ceremony that would be held every year into the foreseeable future, a way of remembering those who died and how they died fighting.

A cold, gusty wind whipped hundreds of American flags near the temporary memorial, and dark clouds covered the sun. Nobody had expected that kind of weather so early in September.

It was rumored that President Bush, who had yet to visit the crash site, would attend the service, and security was intense. State police stood vigil on horseback. Sharpshooters in camouflage lay on their bellies in the grass, behind hay bales, and down in the hemlocks. Jets flew over periodically, and helicopters hovered in and out of the clouds.

At 10:06 A.M., the time of the crash, many family members wept as a huge cast bell tolled forty times while the names of the victims were read.

There was a podium set up with cameras and cameramen. Sandy Dahl, who was fast becoming a spokesperson for Flight 93, addressed the crowd and spoke of the "selfless sacrifice" of the crew and passengers. "In the air, a wave of courage made its way from the cockpit to the rear of the aircraft and back again," she declared, "with all persevering to the end."

Currently, Dahl was no longer flying as a stewardess for United Airlines. She had taken a leave of absence that would stretch into three years as she tried to deal with the sudden loss of the man she loved. But this day she bravely told the families that they could leave Shanksville with the gift of hope—"hope that carries us through tomorrow when the clouds will part and the sun will shine on our lives again."

A strong subtext of the ceremony was the *direct connection* between the passenger revolt and President Bush's newly initiated War on Terror. When Tom Ridge, who had been Pennsylvania's governor at the time of the crash and was now head of the newly created Department of Homeland Security, took the podium, he made no bones about the military significance of the revolt and hailed the forty passengers and crew as "citizen soldiers." Current Pennsylvania governor Mark Schweiker followed Ridge and reinforced the military reference, calling Flight 93 "a battlefield unlike others in our nation's history. . . . It was here that freedom took its first stand."

Those aboard Flight 93 weren't the only ones who were honored. "Today, we also honor and thank a community," said Ridge. "The people of Shanksville embraced the families of Flight 93 as their own. . . . As the sister of one of the passengers said, 'This sleepy little town just puts its arms around you and embraces you.'" With that, almost every one of the family members turned to applaud the surrounding community members. After a moment, the crowd erupted in an answering ovation.

Shortly after noon, President Bush arrived, and the families applauded and gathered to greet him. It was his first visit to the crash site, although he had long since embraced "Let's roll" as a battle cry. Bush and the First Lady bowed their heads as a wreath of roses was laid upon the site and a choir sang "The Battle Hymn of the Republic." Then they greeted the families, with whom the president had become enormously popular. For Bush—as he had often stated in speeches since 9/11—the unity of the passengers and crew prefigured the unity of the country immediately following the terrorist attacks.

A somewhat different note was struck by Muriel Borza, the eleven-year-old sister of Deora Bodley, for whom world peace had been a lifelong wish. She asked the crowd to take a moment to reflect on the prospect of world peace in memory of Deora. The ensuing silence, reported CNN, "was punctured only by the sound of the strong wind blowing across the crash site."

5

IN SEARCH OF
THE "ONE
BRILLIANT IDEA"

One minute before the five o'clock deadline on a cold day in January, a United Airlines flight attendant rushed into the NPS headquarters in Somerset. She was the last of more than a thousand designers or would-be designers who had shipped or hand-delivered their design concepts for the Flight 93 memorial since registration opened in December. Each wanted his or her design to be chosen as the one brilliant idea that would be realized at the crash site to commemorate the heroes of Flight 93.

The flight attendant had made a marathon three-hundred-mile journey down from the Jersey Shore that day with a friend, almost running out of gas en route. When they pulled into Somerset, they parked the car in the wrong direction on a one-way street, just in time for the flight attendant to hustle over to the NPS office.

Her last-minute entry was dedicated to a fellow United Airlines flight attendant who had been on Flight 93. On September 11, they had crossed paths on the runway at Newark International Airport, her flight coming in for a landing just before Flight 93 taxied away. Her design clearly carried a freight-load of emotion, as did many of the 1,011 entries for the memorial. Some of the entrants had never designed anything before, much less a national memorial to an event that changed American history.

The competition was open to everyone, regardless of background or experience—from professional landscape architects to novices who had never drawn anything before in their lives. "It had to be [open]," said Carole O'Hare, a first-stage juror and daughter of passenger Hilda Marcin. "This event affected all of America . . . , and everyone should have the right to participate." Even schoolchildren submitted designs.

78   In the end, an avalanche of designs came from all fifty states and dozens of foreign countries. Quite a few even came from Somerset County. By the end of that January day, cardboard boxes threatened to overwhelm the NPS headquarters.

To avoid favoritism, all entries were anonymous. The competition brief was fairly broad: entrants were to propose a memorial expression, which could range from an individual piece of art to a treatment of the entire site.

As is typical with large, complex competitions, the judging would roll out in two stages. Stage I would winnow the 1,011 entries to five finalists, to be chosen in February. The finalists would be given until July to further refine their design concepts. Stage II would determine the best of the five, which would ultimately go into construction. For the NPS, this process was historic: never before had it designed an entire park via a design competition.

• • •

The design competition was the culmination of years of planning and hard work. In early 2003 the NPS inaugurated an organizational structure for the Flight 93 site. The result was a cluster of groups known as "partners," which would devote their energies to transforming the site into a national memorial.

The operational arm of the partners was the Flight 93 Memorial Task Force, which met for the first time on March 1, 2003. The turnout was impressive, comprising more than eighty family members, locals, first responders, and other regional and national stakeholders, some of them traveling thousands of miles to be there. It was critical to provide the family members, in particular, with active roles in the planning, although that was going to be hard in Somerset County because most family members lived in the San Francisco Bay area or New Jersey. Still, in March 2003, family members traveled from both coasts to the hills of Somerset County.

Bringing the diverse Task Force members under one roof was potentially volatile. "There was an awkward situation," recalls local Task Force member Jerry Spangler, "because you had family members and locals who had had no contact prior to the crash—and they had to build trust."

The slow process of building that trust was reflected in the slowness of some of the planning. For example, the Task Force was charged with crafting a mission statement for the memorial. The process included an online survey; town meetings once a month in or near Shanksville, with family members who lived far away being patched in via conference call; and even trips by committee members to California and New Jersey to meet with families in order to sound out their wishes. In the end, most agreed that the goal of the Task Force should not be "What do we want this memorial to look like?" but rather "What do we want this memorial to mean to people?"

The process took almost a year. Consensus had to be reached for virtually everything, but in the end, all agreed that the memorial should do the following: "honor the heroes of Flight 93; revere the hallowed ground that was their final resting place; remember the events of September 11; express the appreciation of a grateful nation; educate visitors about the context of September 11; and offer a place of comfort, hope, and inspiration."

These were worthy goals, but also rather obvious. That almost a year's effort was required to agree on them testifies to the NPS's dedication to seeking unity and leaving no one out. This reflected the Oklahoma City model; as that city's Phil Thompson had said, nothing is more time consuming than gaining consensus among family members who are in pain.

The slow progress in reaching a consensus was not necessarily a bad thing. One consequence of the current obsession with memorials, some say, is that many memorials are built in fevered haste. The final draft of the mission statement was adopted in July 2004. It would serve as the DNA of the memorial going forward.

Working with the NPS, the Task Force also spent more than a year commissioning studies by engineers and economists, compiling a "cultural landscapes inventory" (standard procedure for NPS properties) that gathered together historical information, existing conditions, and landscape characteristics of the site, to be used in the planning efforts and budget decisions. This also called for 3-D computer models of the site's topography. Based on these studies, the Task Force made a momentous decision: rather than sticking to the area immediately around the crash site, the memorial should encompass 2,200 acres.

This whopping acreage would extend the site to Lincoln Highway, allowing visitors access from a major highway rather than a winding maze of local roads. Moreover, it would protect the "viewshed"—the area seen when standing in and around the impact area—and hence the ability of future generations of Americans "to see the 'battlefield' as it was the day that the battle happened," according to Josh First, a land conservation expert brought in from Harrisburg. The viewshed, said First, had to be protected "in order to insure that this hallowed ground is not eroded by development that is either out of character with the area or that is tastelessly commercial."

But acquiring so much real estate would be expensive, and the initial budget was estimated at between $30 and $58 million. The amount took many locals in this relatively poor county by surprise. Over the next few years, millions would pour in from Washington, D.C., and donors from all over the country. It was a windfall that would transform the county, with mixed results.

· · ·

The 1,011 designs were put on public display in an empty shopping center in Somerset.

Opening the boxes had been an event in itself: NPS staff and volunteers wore masks and full-body HAZMAT suits while opening each entry. It was a sign of the times, with terrorist threats such as the Anthrax mail scare still very fresh in people's minds. Once safely uncrated, however, the designs were hung on tidy frames of unpainted lumber that volunteers had constructed in the empty mall, where the public could view them at will and even leave written comments.

A few of the designs were long on heart, long on imagination, and short on restraint. Some of the more over-the-top entries included "Bury My Heart with Flight 93," which showed forty limestone monuments leading to a thirty-foot-high sculpture of a twenty-three-carat gold heart severed in two. Then there were designs that featured freestanding staircases leading up to heaven, a full-size crashed airplane sticking out of the ground, and a statue of Todd Beamer in a martial arts stance.

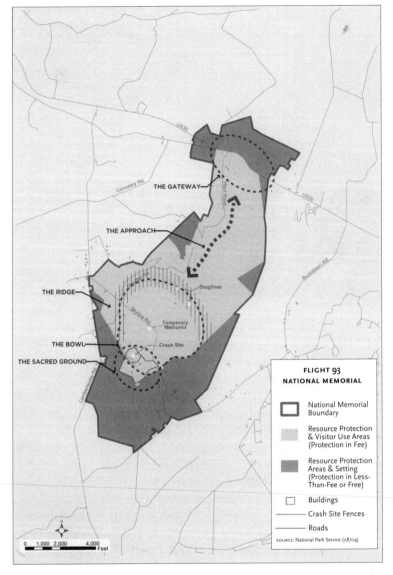

THE GATEWAY

THE APPROACH

THE RIDGE

THE BOWL

THE SACRED GROUND

Draglines

Temporary
Memorial

Crash Site

Cemetery Rd.

Rockwood Rd.

**FLIGHT 93
NATIONAL MEMORIAL**

National Memorial
Boundary

Resource Protection
& Visitor Use Areas
(Protection in Fee)

Resource Protection
Areas & Setting
(Protection in Less-
Than-Fee or Free)

Buildings

Crash Site Fences

Roads

SOURCE: National Park Service (08/04)

0   1,000 2,000   4,000
                            Feet

MAP 3   The 2,200-acre park would allow visitors to access the site from Lincoln Highway and would provide a buffer against offsite development. National Park Service.

Still, these ideas were given equal space in the shopping center with polished designs by degreed architects and landscape architects. "And here's the beauty of it," a regional newspaper exulted. "A Utah housewife has just as much chance of having mapped out the winning design as a world-renowned architect."

That was a polite fiction, of course. The Utah housewife's chances of winning the competition with a sketch she'd drawn on her kitchen table were slim to none, unless she had had architectural or other formal design training or could partner with someone who had. Entrants who lacked such training might have the heart and the reverence for what had happened on board Flight 93, and they might even have the visual imagination to create some eye-catching imagery. But how could their naive design concepts and amateurish drawings prevail over measured, buildable plans and polished presentation boards by trained professionals who spoke the language of design?

• • •

FIG. 10 The Vietnam Veterans Memorial ushered in the era of abstract minimalism in memorial design. Photo: Dewey McLean.

Modern memorial design can be divided into two eras: before and after 1981. That was the year that the design by an undergraduate in architecture at Yale, Maya Lin, was selected for the Vietnam Veterans Memorial.

Prior to this, most memorials featured soaring columns, inspiring inscriptions, or heroic statuary. Take, for example, the Marine Corps War Memorial in Arlington, Virginia, dedicated in 1954. It depicts, in a cast-bronze sculpture thirty-two feet high, a small band of Marines planting a sixty-foot-tall bronze American flag on a mountain on Iwo Jima during World War II. An absolutely literal portrayal of the flag raising, it was based on a photograph taken at the scene. There is no ambiguity in the image and no quibbling about what the memorial celebrates: triumph and the courage of the American fighting men who put their lives on the line to plant Old Glory on this tiny island in the Pacific.

The design for the Vietnam Veterans Memorial represented a complete break from that triumphal tradition. It consisted of a stark black chevron sunk into the earth, completely devoid of ornamentation. Although its black marble walls were inscribed with the names of all those who were killed or went missing in the war, the design was ambiguous in its meaning, if it had any meaning at all. Walking along the sunken pathway, one would see his or her own reflection in the polished marble; the only words inscribed there would be all those names. If the memorial were to mean anything, a visitor would have to construct that meaning for him- or herself.

Maya Lin's stark, unforgiving design sprang from the "less is more" school of twentieth-century art and architecture, which sought to pare forms down to their most basic elements. The logical conclusion of that school was an art movement known as abstract minimalism. It reached its ultimate expression in the 1960s, when artists such as Donald Judd and Robert Morris constructed sculptures consisting of plain walls and boxes.

The supposed advantage of abstract minimalism in memorial design is that it doesn't tell anyone what to think. The Vietnam Veterans Memorial was supposed to be a blank slate on which a visitor could project his or her own narrative, memories, and emotions. Minimalism was also thought to be apolitical, not aligned with a hawkish or dovish or any other partisan agenda, so it was "politically correct" from all points of view.

Or so it was thought. What a surprise, then, that Lin's design ignited a firestorm of controversy among veterans and their supporters. Contrary to the intent to eschew any symbolism in the memorial, many felt that the dark, descending, tomblike walls spoke of doom and defeat—exactly the opposite of the heroic narrative many veterans felt they deserved from their country. Eventually, a kind of compromise was reached by commissioning a lifelike sculpture of three American servicemen, in the heroic tradition, overlooking Lin's wall.

Over time, however, something remarkable happened: the visiting public embraced the Vietnam Veterans Memorial. Perhaps it was the engraved names that moved the visitors more than the design, but the fact remains that the memorial gradually became a sort of shrine. It is the second most visited memorial in the United States, after the Lincoln Memorial. More than that, the Vietnam Veterans Memorial ushered in a new era in memorial design. At the very least, most Americans are no longer shocked by abstract minimalism in the country's memorials.

In fact, minimalism has become the default language of contemporary commemoration. The Vietnam Veterans Memorial paved the way for a spate of others: the Oklahoma City National Memorial

FIG. 11 The World War II Memorial on the National Mall is a traditional memorial that boasts fountains, classical columns, and heroic inscriptions. Photo: Corey Seeman.

(which was directly influenced by the work of Donald Judd), the memorial to the Columbine High School massacre, and the Memorial to the Murdered Jews of Europe in Berlin, to name a few.

These are memorial expressions stripped to their absolute essence—sans heroic inscriptions, sans explicit imagery, sans overt symbolism. An art form that expressed no feeling and (supposedly) carried no message had become the model for memorials to such emotion-laden topics as war, trauma, and tragic death.

• • •

One prominent memorial, however, broke away from that lineage. The National World War II Memorial, just a stone's throw from the Vietnam Veterans Memorial, looks backward to the memorial design that existed in all the centuries before 1981.

Strategically situated between the Washington Monument and the Lincoln Memorial, the World War II Memorial is a seven-acre plaza of white granite framed by triumphal arches and heroic pillars and decked out with bronze eagles, wreaths, and heroic inscriptions. A fountain in the middle of a central pool flings water triumphantly into the air. The overall impression is almost breast-beatingly cele-bratory, leaving a visitor in absolutely no doubt that the American role in World War II was both morally right and one of this country's grandest military achievements. Architecture critics writing in the *Boston Herald*, the *Washington Post*, the *Philadelphia Enquirer*, the *Los Angeles Times*, and other publications almost universally scourged the project for its apparent pomposity and its high-handed imagery, reminiscent of imperial and even fascist regimes. For example, a headline in the *Baltimore Sun* read, "Monument Proposal Draws Criticism: Design's Appearance Called Similar to That of Nazi Ar-chitecture."

It may come as a great surprise, then, that this memorial is one of the most visited and most loved by the American public. It ranks third in visitation in the country, exceeded only by the Lincoln Me-morial and the Vietnam Veterans Memorial, and ahead of the Statue of Liberty, the Washington Monument, the Jefferson Memorial, and every other U.S. memorial.

TripAdvisor, the online travelers' commentary site where anyone can post frank opinions about dingy motel rooms and surly waiters, gave the memorial a certificate of excellence based on 3,037 reviews, many of which are almost rhapsodic. Crowds flock to the memorial, even at night, practically lending it an amusement-park atmosphere.

The fact that this memorial is "the people's choice" despite the critical "thumbs down" points to the chasm between popular and elite taste in America. The Flight 93 leadership sought to bridge the gap between those two worlds in the way it chose the winning entry for the 9/11 memorial.

∎ ∎ ∎

A common process for choosing the design of a memorial involves a design jury, typically made up of design professionals, such as ar-chitects and landscape architects, and professionals from the worlds of art and architectural journalism.

In the closing decades of the twentieth century, however, juries began to include family members and community people who had some stake in the outcome. This was controversial at first. What could lay people with no inkling of the intricacies of design contrib-ute to the process? On the other hand, the old-school "experts" who had historically chosen memorial designs were often out of touch with the visiting public and how it might react to a given design.

Sometimes the experts' avant-garde selection might actually alienate the public—as happened with the Vietnam Veterans Memorial.

In Oklahoma City, civic leaders had been absolutely determined to avoid that kind of alienation. They even went so far as to fire their first competition advisor when he insisted on an experts-only jury. In his stead, they brought in Don Stastny and Helene Fried, facilitators from the West Coast who had experience incorporating community members into design juries to balance the opinions of jurors from the design professions.

Sandra Felt, a Flight 93 family member and stage II juror, agreed that such inclusion was essential. When asked what the family members contributed to the jury, she immediately answered, "The emotional component. And we wanted the memorial to convey emotion."

The NPS, impressed by the Oklahoma City results, brought Stastny and Fried on board to facilitate the process in Shanksville. The jury comprised four nationally known architects and landscape architects, an arts consultant, a design journalist, two family members (one of whom was a high school student), and one NPS regional director. They came from across the country, and all of them, even the family members, had been screened for their ability to arrive at a consensus-driven decision in which personal agendas had no place.

The stage I jury's task was to wade through the thousand-plus memorial entries and winnow just five that might be worth building. They arrived in Somerset on the last weekend in January 2005 for three days of deliberation. Divided into teams, each juror viewed blocks of three hundred or more entries at a time, identifying those worthy of further discussion.

For Sarah Wainio, a family member and high school student who professed a passionate interest in the arts, there wasn't a bad entry in the bunch. "It's incredible to me that so many people put so much time in," she said. But the brutal reality of large design competitions is that almost all the heartfelt efforts must end up on the cutting-room floor if the "one brilliant idea" is to emerge. "On a design jury, you have to have a taste for carnage," a veteran juror once told me. And this jury took its carnage seriously: by the end of the first day of intense deliberations, it had pared the field from 1,011 down to 26.

The next morning, the jurors toured the crash site. A moonscape in the bitter January cold, it had a profound effect on them, especially those who were seeing the place where the plane went down for the first time. Then they returned to the shopping center and deliberated into the evening before cutting the field down to eight.

On the final day, the jury settled on five finalists who would go forward to the stage II competition. The finalist teams would convene in Shanksville the next month for a two-day master-plan workshop to explore the site's resource conditions and ensure that any of the design concepts could be built in accord with the NPS's master plan and requirements for the new park. After the workshop, each finalist team would receive a $25,000 honorarium to refine its design concept and build a three-dimensional scale model.

The amateur designers' stairways to heaven, crashed airliners, and Todd Beamers in martial-arts stance—heartfelt though they may have been—all ended up on the cutting-room floor. After the carnage was done, the simplest ideas survived, and the finalist teams were all led by trained architects or landscape architects, with one graduate student in architecture in the mix. Apparently, you couldn't produce a winning memorial expression on heart alone.

. . .

One frigid day in February 2005, the five finalist teams gathered at the crash site. They came from as far away as California to immerse themselves in the ambience of the place and meet family members and locals. The entire landscape looked like someplace in the Arctic—the land completely white, snow blowing horizontally, and the sky almost as white as the hills.

The youngest finalist was twenty-eight-year-old Ken Lum, a baby-faced Malaysian-born graduate student in architecture at Waterloo University in Toronto. "This is a very humbling site," said Lum as he stood swaddled in his parka. "It overpowers you and makes you feel really small."

There to record Lum's reactions was a Canadian television reporter. A Canadian vying in a major U.S. competition was news in Toronto, and Lum's place among the finalists created a classic David-and-Goliath confrontation. After all, Lum, who still lived at home with his parents, was up against established U.S. designers with impressive credentials. If his design turned out to be the successful one, Lum would repeat the triumph of Maya Lin, another architecture student of Asian descent, who beat out a field of professionals to design the Vietnam Veterans Memorial.

FIG. 12 Ken Lum's design traced the flight path on the landscape. Photo: Ken Lum.

"I never expected this," said Lum. He had only found out about the competition by accident while browsing the Internet. Creating the initial design boards "was more like an exercise," and he was "shocked and actually humbled" to win finalist status, along with the $25,000 honorarium. Now, meeting his competition face to face, he thought, "What am I up against?"

Back in Toronto, Lum evicted his parents from their den at home and turned it into his own design central. He enlisted two other graduate students from Waterloo, Dennis Fanty and Yvonne Lam. They all put aside their master's theses to dedicate themselves full

In Search of the "One Brilliant Idea"

FIG. 13 "Moments of significance" were etched on the roof of Ken Lum's walkway design. Photo: Ken Lum.

time to elaborating and refining Lum's original design concept. The three of them had just 110 days to produce a finished design with illustrative renderings and a scale model that could stand up against the best his professional competitors had to offer.

Lum's concept was to trace the abortive path of Flight 93, which had first headed west toward San Francisco, then suddenly turned back east and south before slicing into the Pennsylvania field. The built result, which he called "(F)Light," was a roofed walkway that would meander across the landscape in the shape of a huge, irregular "V" that mimicked the flight path. Lum's goal was to help visitors experience the events on board the plane as they channeled slowly and deliberately across the landscape toward a point overlooking the sacred ground.

The most notable aspect of the design was the roof structure over the walkway, composed of an outer layer of textured cast glass and an inner layer of laminated glass on quartzite skin, fastened on a structural steel space frame. "Moments of significance" during the flight would be etched into the roof so that the visitor would have to look up at the sky to read the inscriptions. The lighted structure would be visible from an airplane at night. Although Lum proposed positioning rocks quarried from the site along the walkway and re-taining the rusting draglines, the polished and refined materials of his linear roofscape would appear strikingly urban against the rugged landscape of the former strip mine.

With the days rapidly ticking away to turn his initial concept into an award-winning design presentation, Lum added another graduate student to his team: Ivan Ilic, who would focus on building the required three-dimensional model of the design. Even with this addition to the team, there didn't seem to be enough time, and Lum wasn't sleeping much. Five days before the design was due in Pennsylvania, Lum pinned his drawings on the wall of the local library and invited locals to comment. On hand was Siamak Hariri, a prominent Toronto architect and friend of Lum's family. His comments were not encouraging.

"It's way too abstract," said Hariri. "You've got to find a way to communicate it. Does your mother get it? If she doesn't, it's not gonna work."

His comments came as a punch in the gut for Lum, who knew that five days weren't enough to turn his presentation around. The next morning, however, Hariri repented of his bluntness and offered Lum his top designers for those last few days; they would help Lum create computer-aided presentation drawings to visually "sell" the design concept to the jury. They finished the day before the design boards and model were due, and Lum, despite his lack of sleep, had little choice but to hand deliver the materials. So he and Ilic set out on the ten-hour drive across the Canadian border and south to Somerset. They got their entry in just under the wire.

A Canadian television reporter also traveled to Somerset and interviewed Jeff Reinbold, who had succeeded Joanne Hanley as superintendent of the Flight 93 memorial site. "What are the odds of a student from Canada winning a great big U.S. design competition?" the reporter asked.

"As good as any," said Reinbold. "All five designers will be treated very equally. No politics."

■ ■ ■

At the other end of the professional spectrum was an architect from Beverly Hills, California. Paul Murdoch had run his own practice for seventeen years with his wife, Milena, also an architect, after working for architectural gold medalists Charles Moore and Arthur Erikson. He had designed public and academic libraries, university learning centers, gymnasiums, a city hall for South Los Angeles, laboratories, offices, and custom homes.

Murdoch found out about the Flight 93 competition very late in the game, while flipping through an architectural journal. He and Milena had wanted to do something as designers in response to 9/11, so he sent off for the competition brief. When it arrived in early December, they had only a few short weeks to conceive and draw up a comprehensive design that would give them a good shot at being finalists.

Of course there was no time for a site visit, but Murdoch had grown up outside Philadelphia and had camped and canoed in the Laurel Highlands, as the region around Shanksville is sometimes called, so he had some sense of what the area was like. It also helped that the Flight 93 mission statement, included in the brief, looked as though it had been formed through input from different stakeholders; the goals for the project seemed clear.

Murdoch began by asking the key question about any modern memorial: *How much narrative should a memorial have? How much information, as opposed to the memorial evoking certain emotions?* (Ultimately, the Murdochs would decide against information about the crash and in favor of evoking emotion.) He and Milena began sketching and kicking around ideas, and then closed the office for two weeks for the holidays. Again, it was a terribly short time to produce a successful design for an international competition, but they were experienced architects and used to working under pressure.

When asked what other memorials they looked to for design inspiration, Murdoch responded, "None. We found plenty of inspiration in the site itself. And forty citizens fighting back on the terrorists' plane. We felt it was important to focus on these things rather than other memorials."

The Murdochs came out of that two-week holiday period with a design concept they felt good about. "I had a pretty clear idea that I wanted to embrace the sacred ground," said Murdoch. "A kind of national embrace around this field of honor. The field was already a sanctified field. We were not creating something sacred here. It was already there. The design was really a gesture of framing and clarifying the field to heighten and intensify what was already there."

The "embrace" took the form of a crescent of red maples that echoed the semicircular "bowl" of low hills that wrapped around the sacred ground. The other key element from the beginning was the strong linear gesture of the flight path of Flight 93 in its final,

92

FLIGHT 93
NATIONAL
MEMORIAL

A common field one day... A field of honor forever

The Tower of Voices

N

The Sacred Ground

FIG. 14 Paul Murdoch's design featured a crescent of red maples around the bowl of land that partly encircles the crash site, with the line of the flight path slicing across it. Photo: Paul Murdoch Architects.

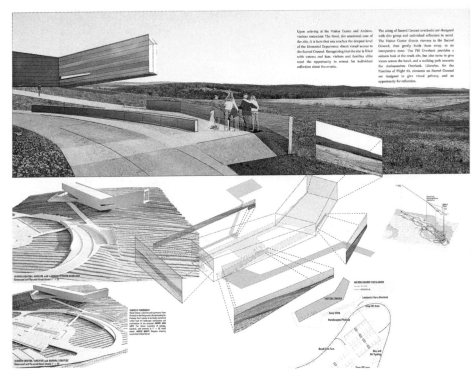

FIG. 15 The Texas team's design featured a visitor center shaped like an airplane cockpit. Photo: Frederick Steiner, Lynn Miller, Karen Lewis, and Jason Kentner.

terrible descent. The Murdochs' initial diagrams, then, portended a starkly simple design, if on a grand scale: a semicircle one-half mile across with the hard line of the flight path slicing through it.

A Murdoch staffer who was a whiz with Photoshop and digital paint techniques imported the Murdochs' sketches in black pen into the computer, together with the photos on the CD that came with the competition brief, and digitally painted over them to create a convincing presentation of what the memorial would look like. "It was important that these evoked the feeling we were after—landscape oriented and very emotional," said Murdoch.

When the Murdochs shipped their presentation board off to the stage I competition, they felt confident about what they'd sent. So Paul Murdoch was delighted, if not completely surprised, to get the news in January that their design was among the five finalists chosen from more than a thousand entries. He quickly began assembling a diverse team of specialists who would give him the very best chance of winning the competition: civil engineers, structural engineers, lighting designers, graphic and typography designers, a security designer, and a cost estimator.

A professional model maker in Los Angeles crafted the architectural models of the site required for the stage II competition. A landscape architect was essential, and Murdoch scoured the East Coast for established landscape offices experienced in rural landscapes as well as formally designed landscapes. He settled on Nelson Byrd Woltz of Charlottesville, Virginia.

The Murdochs' highly professional, team-oriented approach was strategically aimed at winning the stage II competition and ensuring that their design emerged as the "one brilliant idea."

• • •

Another very established finalist was Frederick "Fritz" Steiner, the dean of the School of Architecture at the University of Texas. Together with Lynn Miller, who was in charge of the Master of Landscape Architecture program at the same university, Steiner formed a small team that included Jason Kentner, a young landscape architecture faculty member, and Karen Lewis, a lecturer in architecture at another university.

If there is any aspect of creating disaster memorials that could in any way be called "uplifting," it is the design phase. If the impetus to create such memorials is tragedy and grief, the excitement of giving form to emotions and sketching concepts on big sheets of paper gets designers' juices flowing. Steiner's small team of academics set to work.

Not unlike Lum, they decided to interpret the entire site as a symbolic "journey," which they called the "Memory Trail," though it was a road rather than a walking path. The road rose gently through a field of red maples to views of the sacred ground. Then, like Lum's covered walkway, it took a sharp turn that referenced the jog that Flight 93 made when the terrorists turned the plane toward Washington.

The journey included a visitor center, a funnel-shaped building cantilevered out from the side of the highest point of the site, where it would be visible all the way from Lincoln Highway. Its interior recalled the cramped interior of a jet plane; a visitor would walk up a ramp that provided glimpses of the sky before reaching a "cockpit" that overlooked and framed the crash site. The Texas team made no attempt to blend the white funnel-like structure into the landscape, reasoning that the crash itself didn't "fit" the rural Pennsylvania landscape. It was a bold, in-your-face design element, and the team was taking a big risk with it.

Steiner was called away from a business meeting in Miami to hear the thrilling news that their design had made it to the finals. Back in Austin, the team got to work. They developed a comprehensive design for the site, including the path visitors would follow to the sacred ground, the visitor center, and the parking areas.

In March, Steiner, who hadn't been able to make the February visit to the site with the other finalists, took the opportunity of a business trip to Cleveland to make a pilgrimage there. It was a cold and windy day when he crisscrossed the strip mine–ravaged landscape on local roads. He was struck by the giant draglines on the barren horizon and the temporary memorial with its flags billowing in the March wind. Steiner had seen many photographs of the site and had listened to descriptions of it, but standing on this dread landscape was a very different matter. The place possessed raw power.

Inside the temporary shelter, Steiner met Nevin Lambert, a local farmer who had stood facing Flight 93 as it barreled toward his farmhouse before making its sudden, fatal dive. Now Lambert was serving as an ambassador and was talkative and inquisitive. As a contestant in the competition, Steiner wanted to keep a low profile, but Lambert persisted. When Steiner told him what he hoped to do, Lambert started to cry and hugged him, saying "Thank you, thank you" over and over.

Later that spring, at a workshop in Somerset, each team of finalists got the chance to present its concept. Steiner spoke for the Texas team. As he rose and looked out at the audience, he saw raw emotion in the faces of the family members who awaited his words. He tried not to be distracted by their tears as he described his team's approach.

As the June deadline neared, the Texas team worked day and night to complete their models, boards, and brochures. They had resisted the temptation to add other talent to their small cohort, so they had to do everything themselves. Kentner, for example, built their design models—a considerable task—himself. After a FedEx

FIG. 16 The Lovingers' design featured a "bravery wall" that snaked across the landscape. Photo: Leor Lovinger.

truck picked up the project, Lynn Miller flew to Somerset to unpack the models.

Then Steiner and his cohort waited and waited. They set arbitrary dates for when they expected to hear a verdict, but these dates came and went. One of the younger team members was convinced that they had won, but Steiner felt that the Murdoch team had the strongest entry. Still, he suspected that the Murdochs' central image of a crescent of maples—reminiscent of the crescent symbol of Islam—might be a fatal flaw. His hunch was to prove prescient.

• • •

Finalists Leor and Gilat Lovinger, like Ken Lum, were not American citizens. They had moved to Berkeley, California, from Israel two months before 9/11. Leor had just begun graduate studies in landscape architecture at the University of California, and he and Gilat had started working at a landscape architecture firm on a work visa.

Both felt a profound connection to the aftermath of the terrorist attack. Growing up in Israel, the terrorist threat had been a part of their day-to-day lives, but September 11 was on a totally different scale and Leor felt as shocked as any American citizen. "It was clear to me after 9/11," he said, "that I was going to submit proposals for all the related competitions—in a way, an opportunity to contribute to the discussion of memory, but perhaps also in a more personal manner to heal my hurting soul."

Unlike some of the other finalists, the Lovingers were clear about the design precedents that inspired them: one a contemporary environmental art installation, the other an ancient earthwork fortification. Carl Andre's *Secant* (1977) was a simple line of timbers laid across a field, intended, like Christo's more famous *Running Fence*, to direct the visitor's eye and help him or her see the field in a new way. Hadrian's Wall was, of course, the Roman legions' barrier that stretched across the hills of England to keep the wild tribes of Scotland at bay. The Lovingers' resulting design, "Disturbed Harmony," consisted of a "bravery wall" five feet wide and two and a half miles long. It flowed up and down across the topography, like Hadrian's Wall, telling the story of the forty heroes and leading the visitor to the crash site, while narrating a timeline of events along the way.

Helen Fried of the competition management team caught the couple by surprise late one evening with the news that they had been chosen as finalists. They were touched and humbled by the news, although the timing wasn't the best—Gilat was nine months pregnant. They decided to partner with their employer, the legendary landscape architect Lawrence Halprin of San Francisco, designer of the Franklin D. Roosevelt Memorial in Washington, D.C., and other projects. When the finalists were summoned to Somerset in February, Gilat had just given birth, so Leor flew out to snowy Pennsylvania with the managing principal of Halprin's office. There he was especially moved by the hemlock grove, which seemed to be a very spiritual place, with the dark trunks standing out against the white background. On his return to California, he and Gilat worked with Halprin's office to refine their plans and build the models.

• • •

The only finalist who lived within driving distance of the crash site was Laurel McSherry, who headed up the landscape architecture department at Ohio State University. She took the opportunity, at the very beginning of the competition process, to make the four-hour trip to Shanksville to see the place for herself.

It was a cold day and the wind was blowing hard when McSherry found her way along the back roads to the temporary memorial.

There was no one else there, but plenty of evidence, in the form of personal tributes on the chain-link fence, that people had been there. McSherry was reminded of other spontaneous memorials in the landscape—crosses by the side of the road and such—that, like these, seemed very private expressions in a very public place.

Driving back to Ohio through the Laurel Highlands, McSherry reflected on what she had seen. Her sense was that the task ahead was less about designers reshaping the site and more about how the tradition of the temporary memorial could be carried forward. Back in Ohio, she began sharing ideas with her partner on the project, architect Terry Surjan at Arizona State University. Meanwhile, McSherry tracked down the U.S. Geological Survey maps of the site, all the way back to the time before the land was strip-mined. "There had been so much destruction on that site already," McSherry remembers. "That site had seen so much aggression with machinery, and then the plane crash, so we felt that anything we did on the site should be soft—not bringing in a lot of equipment but working with the site from the inside out."

McSherry and Surjan's design, "Fields Forests Fences," essentially aimed to restore the site to something resembling the pre-mining and pre-crash landscape, using reforestation and other plantings on a vast scale to guide visitors through the site. Positioned along the crest of the bowl and overlooking the sacred ground, a memorial fence, sparsely assembled from posts and wire, would reference both the traditional barbed-wire fence of the farm field and the temporary memorial. Visitors would be given metal tags like the ones foresters use to tag trees, on which they could emboss a simple message; they would hang these on the fence, along with other tributes they brought with them. In this way, the designers would not dictate the form of the memorial; visitors would do that over time, much as they did at the temporary memorial.

Down at the sacred ground, which only family members could enter, forty Stonehenge-like steles would stand in a birch grove—individual gravestones in a common grave. Each stele would be engraved with the name and hometown of the deceased and oriented in the direction of the hometown, so that family members could go to sleep at night knowing that their loved one's headstone was facing them.

Of the five designs that made it to stage II, this one was distinguished as having the fewest built structures and making the least

Memorial Fence with metal forestry tags

①

Hemlocks Belt

②

Marker Urns

FIG. 17 McSherry and Surjan's design involved a massive replanting of the strip-mined site. Photo: Laurel McSherry.

impact on the land. There were no Hadrian's Walls, no overlook plazas, and no replicas of airplane fuselage. "We got as far as we did with having the least formal design," McSherry remarked.

When they received the stunning news that they were among the finalists, McSherry and Surjan expanded their team to include two graduate students from Arizona State, Jason Ploszay and Anson Chen; historic preservation specialist Randall Mason from Maryland; and, perhaps most significantly, Marita Roos and Teresa Durkin, principals of the ecological design firm Andropogon in Philadelphia. Five weeks before the boards and model were due, Surjan and his two students flew to Ohio and worked with McSherry for a month, often late into the night. McSherry drove the project to Somerset just in time to meet the deadline.

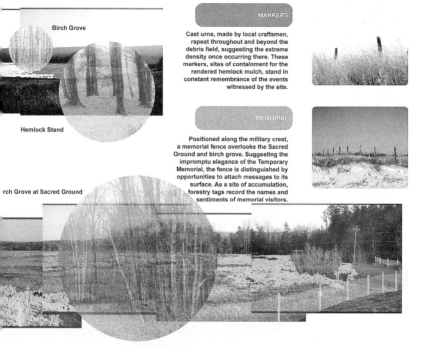

Birch Grove

Hemlock Stand

rch Grove at Sacred Ground

MARKERS

Cast urns, made by local craftsmen, repeat throughout and beyond the debris field, suggesting the extreme density once occurring there. These markers, sites of containment for the rendered hemlock mulch, stand in constant remembrance of the events witnessed by the site.

MEMORIAL

Positioned along the military crest, a memorial fence overlooks the Sacred Ground and birch grove. Suggesting the impromptu elegance of the Temporary Memorial, the fence is distinguished by opportunities to attach messages to its surface. As a site of accumulation, forestry tags record the names and sentiments of memorial visitors.

But how would their "design with nature" approach fare with the stage II jury? "Above all other entries," wrote one critic in Pittsburgh, "this one respects the land but does not go far enough in interpreting the events of 9/11 and honoring the crew and passengers."

• • •

The stage II jury, which had the monumental burden of choosing the one definitive design for a national memorial to an event that changed American history, met in early August. It was more family-heavy than the stage I jury, with eight family members, two locals, five design professionals, and one NPS regional director.

Sandra Felt, the wife of Flight 93 passenger Edward Felt, was one of the family members. She was not overly excited about the idea of a memorial per se. Like many of the families, she would have preferred to leave the crash site—the cemetery of her husband—undisturbed.

Her main concern was that his resting place not be vandalized. "A gravestone, a fence, and a 'no trespassing' sign—that would have been fine with us," she told me.

So why couldn't they have had something that simple? "Public pressure," she said. "You have to accommodate the public. The train has left the station and what are you going to do—stand in front of it? So from day one I promised my daughters I would do as much as I could to participate to see that there was a memorial."

Henry Cook, president of the Somerset Trust Company, was one of the locals on the jury. He was taken aback when he was invited to serve because he knew so little about architecture and design and made no bones about it. He suspected that his inclusion was the result of a last-minute decision to involve a local—any local. The jury process would turn out to be the most intense four days that Cook had ever spent.

Cook's office is on the top floor of the Trust building in uptown Somerset. His family has been in Somerset County since the 1830s, and he's the fifth generation of his family to run this bank. Cook has deep Pennsylvania roots, and he finds it significant that "to contemplate the American Revolution, we go to Valley Forge, to contemplate the Civil War, we go to Gettysburg, to contemplate the War on Terror, we come to Shanksville—and the irony of this is that the three wars that were fought on American soil are best remembered in Pennsylvania."

Cook had no preconceptions of what the Flight 93 memorial should look like. But he did have an inkling of what its purpose should be: it was "for Americans to contemplate the price of freedom in an open society. Because freedom is very, very expensive, and Flight 93 is the price side."

To prepare himself as much as possible, Cook read a couple of books about how America memorializes events and went to Washington, D.C., to see a national memorial for himself. The memorial he chose to visit—the baroque World War II Memorial on the National Mall—turned out to be an ironic choice. Whichever design the stage II jury selected, it would be a very different animal.

. . .

Like the stage I jury, the jurors began by driving to and across the crash site as a future visitor might experience it—from Lincoln Highway across the ridge and down into the bowl, at the center of which

Flight 93 had crashed. Along the way they viewed the temporary memorial, the former Rollock scrap yard buildings, and finally the sacred ground.

Most of the jury members were on the land for the first time, and all were awestruck by the seeming tranquility of the place that, a few years earlier, had witnessed the deaths of forty people, murdered in the most violent way possible. How would a successful memorial fit in with this intimidating site? They then went back to Somerset and began reviewing the five designs. After an in-depth analysis of each—first alone, then in small groups—each juror shared what he or she felt were important criteria going forward. Some of their comments were recorded anonymously.

"The Memorial should confront the issues. Terrorism is ugly—to make the Memorial too serene may be missing the point."

"The Memorial should evoke emotion, but avoid emotional cliché."

"The Memorial must speak to, and be understood by, the common citizen—not be an intellectual exercise."

"Those family members that are on the Jury must be objective in our evaluation, but we should also honor the passion we all feel as to what this place means and the story it tells."

"The determination of the Memorial design should be based not only on today's needs, but the needs one hundred years from now. How will the story of the 40 and their actions be told then?"

In the first two days of intense discussion, the jury further narrowed down the finalists. Most designs were seen to possess some fatal flaw. "Fields Forests Fences" was praised as a bold, minimalist design, but its interpretation of Flight 93 seemed so subtle that the interpretation itself needed interpreting. "Disturbed Harmony" might be more easily understandable, but some jurors felt that the two-and-a-half-mile-long wall was monotonous. "(F)Light" was thought to come closest to allowing the visitor to experience what the forty felt when they acted, but some jurors wondered whether the sophisticated architecture of the linear walkway would overshadow the experience of the site itself. The Texas team's funnel-shaped lookout structure died for much the same reason.

Again and again jurors returned to Paul Murdoch's design, "Crescent of Embrace." The heart of the design—a nine-hundred-foot-long memorial wall—was disarmingly simple. There were no faces of passengers and crew, no sculptures of airplanes, no inscriptions

interpreting the event—just a long walk on which a visitor could view the sacred ground up close and create his or her own narrative about what happened there. It was memorial design stripped to its bare essentials.

"It looks like a diet meal," said Cook. "I don't see where the emotional meat is." He'd been hoping for something so amazing that everybody's jaw would drop. "What we were commemorating was so core to the American experience," he reflected in hindsight, "that probably no design could have lived up to that expectation."

For Sandra Felt, however, the minimalism of the design was a plus—because, again, family members wanted minimal alteration of their loved ones' resting place. There was also the brute fact that, as she put it, "the land has sustained enough." It had been degraded, first by strip mining, then by the murder of forty people. To her, the Murdoch design seemed to lie the lightest on this battered site.

By the end of the last day, emotions were running high as the moment of truth approached. Calvin Wilson, who was present as a member of the Design Oversight Committee, suspected that he felt more jittery than the jury members who actually had to make the decision. After all, the baby was about to be delivered!

But the jurors kept going back and forth. They narrowed the field to two, and then there was another hour's discussion, and then— they picked it.

"['Crescent of Embrace'] best addresses the interface between the public realm of the visitor and private realm of the Sacred Ground while keeping the focus on the content, not on words or imposed symbolism," wrote the jury recorder. "The design is a simple and beautiful expression." Its stripped-down minimalism turned out to be a virtue. As one jury member put it, "This is not a 19th-century memorial. We entered the 21st century when Flight 93 crashed."

• • •

There was one lurking problem with the "Crescent of Embrace": the unintended reference to religious iconography. A local preacher had noticed this at the shopping center where the entries were displayed and had left an angry note protesting what he saw as an homage to Islam. The potential for trouble was not lost on the jury.

"Consider the interpretation and impact of words within the context of this event," the jury wrote in its report. "The 'Crescent' should be referred to as the 'circle' or 'arc' or other words that are not tied to specific religious iconography." Acting on that advice immediately might have avoided serious trouble later on.

• • •

Choosing a winning finalist was a great step forward in constructing a permanent memorial, but it was effectively a death sentence for the temporary memorial, for which Paul Murdoch made no allowance in his site plan. Architects typically see their job as creating places with consistency, form, and structure, and Murdoch's evaluation of the temporary memorial—"there is not really much of a form out there"—was indisputable. The days of "the people's memorial," with its chain-link fence and cluttered, though heartfelt, tributes, were numbered. Such, however, is the curse of all temporary memorials— they can be obliterated at will by those who control the site.

Around Shanksville, opinions about the winning design were mixed. Some residents approved, calling it a fitting tribute to the forty passengers and crew, a memorial that embraced a graveyard. Others feared that the minimalist memorial wouldn't offer the emotional tug of the temporary memorial. Ed Klein, a Shanksville ambassador, believed that symbols of faith, such as crosses hung on the chain-link fence, brought order out of the chaos that was Flight 93. "If it is secularized and sanitized," he said. "I don't know if I will be involved."

Some critics took exception with Murdoch's bare minimalism. "We don't need giant statues of the guys ramming the drink cart into the door," wrote architectural commentator James Lileks. "But pedantic though such a monument might be, future generations would infer the plot." Of the critical response, Christopher Hawthorne observed, "The Hallmark-card Minimalism that is now the lingua franca for memorials—and the design world's version of political correctness—has clashed with the notion that what we ought to remember about its passengers, above all else, is their onboard rebellion." Murdoch's design, for some critics, was altogether "too reflective—too abstract, in a word—to do justice to the legacy of Todd Beamer and the other passengers who joined him in charging the cockpit."

Despite such criticisms, when Murdoch unveiled the winning design at the U.S. Chamber of Commerce, fewer than a thousand feet from the White House, it was a heady moment. Many in the audience, including family members, rose to cheer and applaud. "Optimistically," said Hamilton Peterson, president of the organization Families of Flight 93, "groundbreaking could occur within a year or two."

His optimism was to prove grossly unwarranted.

6

THE MANY FACES
OF MEMORY

We tend to think that a site becomes a memorial by the act of building something on it, usually a massive, enduring structure of stone
and mortar. But in fact—as Abraham Lincoln pointed out in his
Gettysburg Address—the site itself, and what happened there, is
sometimes far more compelling than anything else that can be done
or said. Nor should the response to a mass disaster necessarily be
imposing a structure of stone and mortar. As examples, let's look at
two very different responses to mass disasters, coincidentally within
the general geographic region of Shanksville, a few years after 9/11.

In a small Amish community 180 miles due east of Shanksville,
tragedy struck in 2006. An armed and deranged neighbor entered
the one-room community school and, after ordering the boys and
adults to leave, opened fire on the ten girls who remained, killing
five and leaving the others critically wounded. He then shot himself
as police stormed the building.

The reaction of the deeply religious community was as swift as it
was contrary to anything we might expect from mainstream America. The parents of the slain girls went to the family of the man who
had killed their children that night and forgave him for what he had
done.

And what kind of memorial did the Amish community erect to mark the tragedy? None. In fact, they demolished the schoolhouse where the massacre took place. Strange as this may seem in an era of feverish memorial building, obliteration, as Kenneth Foote has documented, is the traditional fate for sites of mass murder. Most communities simply can't bear any physical reminder of such events.

In the same year, three hundred miles south of Shanksville in the Shenandoah Valley, a Virginia Tech senior with a history of mental instability purchased automatic pistols at a Virginia gun show. One morning he entered classrooms and started firing, killing thirty-two people and wounding seventeen others in two separate attacks before committing suicide. It was the deadliest school shooting by a single gunman in U.S. history.

The massacre left the Virginia Tech community in shock. Nevertheless, that very evening a group of students found an outlet for their grief by creating a spontaneous memorial to those who had died that terrible day. Unlike most immediate responses, however, these students used durable materials, not a pile of cut flowers and teddy bears. They went out to the local quarry and came back with thirty-three rough chunks of limestone, locally called "hokie stones," which they arranged in a semicircle in front of the campus administration building. In an extraordinary gesture of inclusion, they placed a stone for the shooter fourth from the left.

Lincoln spoke of how those who died had "hallowed" the battlefield at Gettysburg. Is it possible that a single spontaneous gesture that grows out of pain and grief, such as the students' laying hokie stones, can hallow the site of a tragedy?

Even the hokie stone left for the shooter sparked heartfelt responses. In the following days, a few students left notes addressed to him. "I hope that if I ever meet anyone like you I will have the courage and strength to reach out and change his or her life for the better," wrote one person, who signed his name as Dave. "I hope the anger towards you that resides in so many hearts turns to forgiveness."

The university administration apparently understood that no formal memorial it could erect would be more fitting than the rough memorial that the students laid down that day. So, rather than putting up a conventional memorial, the university simply replaced the rough hokie stones with dressed blocks of limestone engraved with the names of the dead. They were arranged in the same semicircle

in front of the administration building, but with a strange, sad twist: there were only thirty-two stones—none to memorialize the shooter.

The Virginia Tech massacre sparked another, less conventional response: some of the survivors of the massacre and their supporters decided to take constructive action to prevent such a massacre from ever happening again in Virginia. A loophole in the state's gun-purchase laws allows anyone—including people with a history of mental instability, such as the Virginia Tech shooter—to purchase whatever firearms they wish at any Virginia gun show. Virginia Tech survivors and gun-control advocates poured into the state capitol in Richmond to support a bill to close the loophole. To publicize their advocacy, supporters staged a "lie-in" outside the capitol to draw attention to gun deaths in Virginia that year.

Did the bill pass? It did not, despite the support of Virginia governor Tim Kaine. Among other reasons for denying the bill, Virginia legislators said that closing the gun loophole would hurt business at gun shows. Nonetheless, the Virginia Tech lie-in, however brief, was a memorial in itself and one alternative way of remembering mass tragedies. It, and the Amish community's response, reminds us that a massive stone-and-mortar memorial is not the only response to a mass tragedy. Some of the most powerful memorials are the simplest, and some of the most effective memorials are direct responses to pain.

• • •

A far more contemporary way of remembering Flight 93 emerged in 2005 from the film industry. In fact, Flight 93 inspired two made-for-television movies—the Discovery Channel's *The Flight That Fought Back* and A&E Network's *Flight 93*. Finally, in April 2006, Universal Studios released a major Hollywood film, *United 93*. All called up the memory of the flight, not with inert stone and mortar, but with stomach-churning action and dialogue.

Paul Greengrass, who wrote and directed *United 93*, went the extra mile to involve the families early in the process, and many family members attended screenings in Newark and the suburbs of San Francisco, despite the anguish of watching their loved ones' final minutes portrayed with excrutiating realism. The filmmakers used considerable artistic license, since no one knows in detail much of what took place on board the plane. It is not even known for sure whether the passengers breached the cockpit, although the film shows this happening. Yet the depiction of the passenger revolt again raised the question, Who, really, were the heroes? As Greengrass sat with the cast in the reconditioned Boeing 757 that was used as the set, his eyes immediately went to the youngest and strongest men, and he came to believe that they propelled the passenger rebellion.

In the film, Jeremy Glick, a big, powerfully muscled man, leads a single file of the most athletic male passengers by sprinting down the aisle and kicking a hijacker to the floor. The same men go on to storm the cockpit. While stewardesses attempt to produce makeshift weapons, including boiling water from the galley, there is no question that those spearheading the revolt are a handful of the strongest males.

Family members clashed over the issue at one meeting with Greengrass. Alice Hoagland, however, who was convinced that her rugby-playing son helped lead the attack, agreed with Greengrass, maintaining that only some of the passengers were heroes. To insist otherwise, Hoagland said, "does a disservice to their memory and the truth." Other family members remained dead set on portraying all of the passengers and crew as heroes, and the discussion got so heated that a few family members stormed out of the room.

Greengrass, of course, had the last word. "You cannot divide this experience into forty equal parts," he told the families.

But releasing a major Hollywood film on a still-raw subject ignited a debate that went beyond the families: Was Universal Studios just exploiting a terrible event for commercial gain? Was it unseemly soon for American audiences to see that harrowing plane ride depicted on the big screen? "The jury's still out," said Jeff Dishart, a United Airlines pilot. "In its worst expression, this movie was voyeurism and a possibly—if you'll give me the license—pornographic look at the events. Too intrusive."

Film critic Bob Mondello, too, suspected that the release of the film was inappropriately soon. Seeing the film himself completely changed his mind. "Powerful doesn't begin to describe the film's impact," wrote a converted Mondello. "A couple of weeks ago, the argument that artists should wait to tell this story made sense to me. It no longer does. Wait and you create something for people who no longer really remember that morning. . . . And as we reduce that tragic day to politics and memorials, we are starting to forget."

In the end, *United 93* turned out to be one of the most critically acclaimed films of the year. Universal Studios, which had pledged 10 percent of the first weekend's ticket sales to the Flight 93 memorial, turned over $1.14 million to the Families of Flight 93.

• • •

Out on Stutzmantown Road, Father Al's chapel—that "other" built memorial—was in its fourth year of operation by 2006. Although not "official"—that is, not authorized by the U.S. government—it bore testimony to what a single individual can create (with substantial philanthropic support, of course). In fact, it may go down as one of the most extraordinary *personal* memorial expressions in U.S. history. Even Flight 93 family members contributed artifacts from their loved ones' lives to be displayed there.

On hand to greet every visitor was Father Al. An energetic, garrulous man with combed-back gray hair, he loved meeting the bus tours. Typically he wore not priestly garb but jeans and a T-shirt, and when he recounted the story of the passenger revolt, he often wept.

For Father Al, as for so many touched by the crash of Flight 93, the *duty of memory* was a moral imperative. "Probably the worst fate we

FIG. 20 The United Airlines monument at Father Al's chapel directs visitors in what to feel and think. Photo: Fred Jordan.

could face," he told an interviewer, "is to be forgotten, to be a nothing, to have no one remember you, to have no one to pray for you, to have no one rejoice that your life meant something. Because once you're gone, who will speak for you except those who come after you?"

Remembering the heroes of Flight 93 had become the whole point of his life. He never took a day off. He was at the chapel every day of the week, every week of the year, except once for a few days when his brother was dying and once when he took a trip to Texas to see a ballet commemorating 9/11. He freely admitted that he was obsessed—and apparently had never been happier. "I don't have any life to speak of," he said. "The chapel is everything. I don't have any interest in anything else."

Inside the chapel, with its grandiose chandeliers and other decor, the walls were festooned with mementos donated in remembrance of the passengers and crew. The sign, now famous, that Judi Baeckel had put up in her yard the day after 9/11—"Shanksville Salutes the Heroes of Flight 93"—was mounted along one wall. Some of the donated objects seemed a little cultish. For example, there was a model airplane that Flight 93 copilot Leroy Homer made when he was eleven, together with a pair of plastic gloves that his mother asked visitors to put on before touching it—her son's DNA and fingerprints were still on it.

A tiny meditation room at the front of the church, lit by candles, contained photographs and personal biographies of each passenger and crew member. Father Al said that some people spent hours inside the room, reading every single word.

On September 11, 2006, the chapel received a major enhancement: a black granite monument dedicated to the Flight 93 crew. The CAUSE Foundation, which supports United Airlines crew members, had commissioned the monument and originally offered to place it at the crash site, but the NPS declined it on the grounds that if it accepted every tribute that was offered, the crash site would quickly become a hodgepodge of tributes. Father Al, by contrast, was only too happy to donate land for the monument. United crew members from all over the country, including Sandy Dahl, came to the inauguration.

Each of the crew members' portraits and names were etched in marble, and a polished replica of an airliner seemed to be taking off from the top of the black granite structure. Sited in a formal plaza behind the chapel, it was surrounded by benches with passengers' names engraved in them. Everything was of the finest materials and craftsmanship. Still, compared to the stripped-down, contemporary design of the "Crescent of Embrace," the crew monument was decidedly old-fashioned. It stood bolt upright and was didactic and unabashedly celebratory. Visitors were left in absolutely no doubt as to what to think or feel about the valiant United Airlines crew.

For all its enhancements, Father Al's chapel had one major flaw: its day-to-day operations were completely dependent on Father Al's unflagging energy. No one like Maggie Hardy Magerko, who had made the initial donation to renovate the building, had stepped forward with a revenue stream to keep the place open, and Father Al had to ask for a donation from every visitor and peddle Flight 93 caps, a replica of the chapel, and other souvenirs.

But there was a bigger threat hanging over Father Al's head, and in 2007 it came crashing down on him. Bishop Adamec, who had previously warned him, "Either you go or the chapel goes," reached the end of his tether. The issue was the performing of the Catholic Mass, which Father Al, as a priest unassigned to any church, was prohibited from doing at the chapel or anywhere else. For almost five years Father Al had respected this prohibition, until an unusual temptation came his way. An archbishop of the North American Old Roman Catholic Church, an offshoot of the Catholic Church not recognized by the Vatican, stopped by to perform Mass, and Father Al couldn't resist joining him. When Bishop Adamec got wind of this, he laid down the worst possible punishment for any Catholic priest: he excommunicated Father Al.

Trying to put the best spin on his defrocking, Father Al said, "I realized [Bishop Adamec] didn't punish me, he set me free. I could do the same things I ever did but without him and the church hanging over me. And I still have some work to do."

∎ ∎ ∎

Next to Father Al, Terry Butler is the person in Somerset County whose life has been most profoundly reshaped by the crash of Flight 93. His primary personal memorial is his own body: tattoos cover both arms from wrist to shoulder, and he cut off the sleeves of his shirts for all the world to see the tattoos. I came to see Butler at his workplace, Stoystown Auto Wreckers on Lincoln Highway, where Butler's specialty is removing windshields from wrecked vehicles. He is a powerfully built man with bright blue eyes and a graying ponytail, and when I showed up at the wrecking yard, he readily agreed to talk to me at the end of his shift. I got into his old van, and Butler drove it down the rutted dirt tracks of the wrecking yard, past acre after acre of carcasses of battered automobiles. Driving, it seemed, made it easier for him to talk about how Flight 93 had changed him.

Butler got his first tattoo less than a year after the crash. "It was only supposed to be one tattoo," he said, "and then it just evolved into all this—artwork." Tattoos commemorating 9/11 are not at all uncommon, as Jonathan Hyman documented in *The Landscapes of 9/11: A Photographer's Journey*. Butler's tattoos reflect the standard

114

FIG. 21 Terry Butler's tattoos constitute his own personal memorial. Photo: Mark Pynes. Used with the permission of Pennlive.com © 2014. All rights reserved.

vocabulary of these tattoos: a fireman and a crying Statue of Liberty, along with imagery unique to Flight 93, including a pair of eyes over a description of what Butler saw in the plane's final dive.

Even the discomfort of the tattoo process was welcome because it brought him closer to the Flight 93 victims. "You've got to take pain," he says. "Forty people took pain."

"I just don't want people to forget" is Butler's mission and mantra, even though his own memories seem to cause him a lot of grief. Helplessly viewing the final descent of Flight 93, it seems, left a deep emotional scar. Our conversation took place more than a decade after the crash, but his voice still cracked and his eyes welled up with tears when he talked about it.

"I'm always told we are supposed to move ahead and try to forget," Butler told me, "but I don't know how. I saw it right there." He pointed to the bright blue sky where the 757 streaked diagonally over the wrecking yard. He still tenses up when airliners bound for Pittsburgh fly over. "I don't think I'll ever get over this," he said.

Like Father Al, Butler admits that his extreme focus on Flight 93 may fill an internal need: "I don't have much of anything else." Even

The Many Faces of Memory

a blue pickup truck he has at home serves as a mobile memorial to Flight 93, featuring the words "Let's Roll" boldly emblazoned alongside the forty victims' names and a painted angel. Butler has consecrated his life to ensuring that everyone he meets remembers Flight 93.

• • •

A song performed at Father Al's chapel led to a living, breathing memorial—a dance choreographed in Texas.

For the dedication of the crew monument at the chapel, United Airlines flight attendants congregated from all over the country to form a choir to commemorate the event. The choir sang "A Prayer for Our Time," a hymn written by religious composers Joseph and Pamela Martin in the week following 9/11. One of the singers in the choir was Alicia Sommer, a United flight attendant from the Texas Hill Country who had a background in professional dance.

Sommer had been on vacation in Australia on 9/11. That happenstance likely saved her life, because she regularly flew the Newark to San Francisco route for United—in fact, she had worked that flight just three days before 9/11. It was a chillingly close call for Sommer, and the crash had taken the life of someone close to her—her Newark roommate Sandra Bradshaw, who had been among the crew of Flight 93 that fateful day.

Sommer came back to the United States with a burning desire to channel her shock and grief into some way of ensuring that no one would forget Flight 93, ever. As it happened, she was the artistic director of a dance program in her local Texas community, and her part in the choir at Father Al's chapel inspired her to choreograph a ballet based on the same hymn. She tapped eight teenage dancers in her dance program to perform "A Prayer for Our Time" in a local high school auditorium in May 2007. Sommer's choreography interpreted the sequence of events on 9/11 with dance formations depicting the flight paths of the four airliners; the ballet culminated with the dancers climbing a ladder, representing all the souls who, she believed, went to heaven that day.

Sitting in the high school auditorium was Father Al, who had come to Texas at Sommer's invitation—one of the very few times he took any time off from his chapel. At the end of the dance, he mounted the stage, where the local newspaper photographed him in his priestly cassock with the troupe.

As a memorial, the ballet was a very local event, but it was captured on video by Sommer's husband, Mark, a professional videographer. He sent a copy to every Flight 93 family and to President Bush. Father Al showed the video to every group who visited his chapel. Via current technology, an ephemeral dance performance became a video memorial to the flight.

. . .

Participatory memorial ceremonies found their way to the crash site as well. These included a Flight 93 flag created by Gene Stilp, a fireman who lived near Harrisburg, Pennsylvania. Annual or semiannual ceremonies honoring Flight 93 were "not enough," said Stilp. "The sacrifice and heroics of the passengers and crew need to be remembered every day."

So Stilp created his own memorial to help Americans remember: a flag with fifty stars encircling the number 93. The stripes read, "Our Nation Will Eternally Honor the Heroes of Flight 93." Stilp thought the Flight 93 flag should be flown every day at locations throughout the country. And every year on September 11, he brought a full-size, folded flag to the crash site. At ten minutes before the hour, every hour, he made his way through the crowd in search of people to help him unfold it. "Please, come help me with the flag," he said. "Would you like to help? Please, we need you, come."

When he had gathered forty people of all ages and backgrounds, he lined them up in two rows facing each other and asked them to help unfurl the flag as they looked around at their neighbors. "You came here as strangers," he said. "Now, you've helped do something together. Think about those people on Flight 93. They were strangers too. But, they worked together and saved the next probable targets in Washington, D.C."

Holding tightly to the unfurled flag, the group would stand in silence or sing "God Bless America." As they refolded the flag, each participant would thank the person next to him. This ceremony of memory would be repeated on the hour all day long every September 11th.

. . .

Flight 93 also inspired musical compositions. In addition to Derrill Bodley's sublime "Steps to Peace," the passenger revolt inspired songs in a schmaltzier vein, such as Kristy Jackson's "Little Did She Know (She Kissed a Hero)," which tells the story of an unnamed Flight 93 passenger and the wife he had left at home that morning:

> *Little did she know she'd kissed a hero*
> *Though he'd always been one in her eyes*
> *But when faced with certain death*
> *He'd said a prayer and took a breath*
> *And led an army of true angels in the sky*

Even superstar Neil Young was moved to record a song, "Let's Roll," which expressed the adulation many Americans felt for the passenger revolt. But Young's admiration for the passengers and crew did not extend to the commander in chief. Four years into Bush's wars in Afghanistan and Iraq, Young would record a sequel to "Let's Roll": "Let's Impeach the President."

· · ·

For many of the families, memorializing their loved ones continued to be a path through grief. The methods by which they did so suggest just how variable the idea of a memorial can be.

Larry and Barbara Catuzzi looked for ways to remember their daughter Lauren through good works in her memory. Larry, an investment banker in Houston, set up the Lauren Catuzzi Grandco-las Foundation and convinced power brokers in Houston to allow the foundation to build a garden in a public park and dedicate it to Lauren. "Lauren's Garden," located in Market Square Park in the heart of downtown Houston, now includes a fountain and a cast-bronze bust of Lauren surrounded by flowerbeds. Meanwhile, Lauren's sisters, Vaughn and Dara, took on an idea that she had been working on when she died—a book of self-empowering ideas and advice for women. They saw to it that the book, *You Can Do It!*, was completed and published by Chronicle Press.

The foundation also contributed toward birthing rooms at hospitals. One birthing room was located at Marin General Hospital in California, where Lauren, who was three months pregnant at the time she was killed, would likely have had her baby. Sometimes, on September 11, her husband, Jack, would honor her memory by stopping by the birthing room and asking how many babies had been born there that year. The foundation's good works were, in effect, memorials.

Such well-meaning efforts did not bring healing to all family members. They certainly didn't heal Sandy Dahl, despite her efforts to find creative ways of keeping her husband's memory alive. With friends and neighbors, she established a scholarship fund in Jason's name to help young pilots pay for their education. She started giving speeches about the heroism of those on Flight 93, even though the role of spokesperson was hard for her because it kept calling up how Jason died.

Despite all her efforts to find constructive outlets for her grief, Dahl remained stuck in the grieving process, unable to come to terms with her loss and to somehow move ahead with her life. A beautiful woman, Dahl had not remarried. She kept Jason's twisted and broken keys and his charred logbook, which were recovered after the crash; she treasured these things even though they reminded her of the horror of Jason's last moments. She still lived in the house near Denver that Jason had been renovating. It was a big house, and it wasn't finished. And she was alone. Some nights, she awoke from nightmares. Even after she was diagnosed with post-traumatic stress disorder, she clung to the afflictive memory of her loss, the only link that still bonded her to the man she loved.

"Closure," in the sense of "moving on" or "getting over it," is a term that those with direct experience of tragedy, such as Wally

Miller, view with great skepticism. "A lot of people talk about getting closure," said Miller. "There is no closure when there's sudden death. There may not be closure when there's any death. A large hole has been torn into these people's lives. It will never be filled."

Ed Linenthal's many interviews with the bereaved in Oklahoma City had left him, too, with a deep distrust of terms such as "the healing process," as if there were a regular set of steps through which people move and, in the end, emerge happy. Those he interviewed bitterly resented this kind of language. It represented a failure to recognize the magnitude of the evil that had been done. An event like the Murrah Federal Building bombing could coil back on itself and erupt in different ways. How disrespectful to approach a mother of a murdered child in Oklahoma City and say, "Well, now it's ten years later. Have you reached closure?"

Memory, Linenthal concluded, *is not, by definition, healing.*

Cathy Stefani, mother of passenger Nicole Miller, also found herself locked in an iron cage of grief. The *San Francisco Chronicle* reported that, five years after the crash, she maintained Nicole's bedroom exactly as she had left it, even keeping the voicemail Nicole had left on the answering machine before boarding Flight 93. For the first two years after 9/11, Stefani was so grief-stricken—despite the fact that she still had a husband and two other children—that she was on and off disability leave from her job. Every day, she'd sit in her daughter's room and cry. When Stefani still hadn't dismantled Nicole's bedroom after five years, friends asked, "Isn't it time to get over it?" "No," Stefani would always answer. "This is something that should never be forgotten . . . and I will never get over it. And I don't think any of the families will."

"Survivor guilt" was a fallout of the crash for Kim Stroka, who was, like Sandy Dahl, a United Airlines stewardess. She had been scheduled to fly on Flight 93 but had taken the day off, and she experienced intense guilt about the death of the stewardess (whom she did not identify) who had taken her place. She now experienced panic attacks when a plane flew over her house and began shaking when someone drove her to the airport. She ended up quitting her job as a stewardess for United and still needed years of therapy.

Flying had also become fearful for family member Carole O'Hare, but for a different reason: she was afraid of anyone who looked Middle Eastern, such as the two men she sat next to on a flight to New

York, who had no carry-on luggage. "I was scared to death," O'Hare said. "I'm almost ashamed of it because I don't try to profile people." An odd corollary to O'Hare's experience was that, at a party following the premiere of *United 93*, none of the Flight 93 relatives spoke to the actors who played the hijackers.

Derrill Bodley, who had lost his beloved daughter Deora in the crash, also continued seeking a path through grief through good works—in this case, working for peace. He had made another trip to Afghanistan and come back to work on "Eyes Wide Open," a Quaker traveling exhibit that displayed a pair of boots in a public place for every American killed in the war in Iraq.

His crusade to remember Deora through good works ended abruptly on his sixtieth birthday, when he crashed his motorcycle while returning home from an errand. His journey in memory of his daughter was over. He wouldn't even make it to the peace rally he had planned to attend in Washington, D.C., the following weekend.

• • •

Not all of the Flight 93 families wanted a built memorial. Beatrice Guadagno, mother of Richard Guadagno, said that building a memorial "was never a big issue for me. I know where my son is. I know where his remains are going to be forever. I don't have to have a memorial for him. When I go there, I sit on his bench, which I love. The important thing is Shanksville and just sitting there with my own memories and looking out on that field."

Sometimes the simplest and most ephemeral expressions, such as gazing out over hallowed ground, are the most effective ways of honoring a memory.

• • •

In 2006 the NPS initiated a massive project that would constitute a different kind of memorial: an oral history archive that would gather verbatim face-to-face interviews with family members, first responders, and anyone else who had a story to tell about the aftermath of the crash and their journey thereafter. The oral histories, which are still being compiled at this writing, would eventually number in the hundreds. Kathie Shaffer, a Shanksville native, was hired by the NPS to conduct the majority of them.

Conducting the interviews could be heartrending. Voicing the sadness of their losses could wring bitter tears even from strong men. One of these was Calvin Wilson, the brother-in-law of Flight

93 copilot LeRoy Homer. Wilson cried as he told the story of his first visit to the crash site.

"As weird as this may sound," said Wilson, "my first day, when I turned, there were forty people standing there."

He'd walked into the hemlock grove, and when he turned around, there they were—the passengers and crew of Flight 93. They seemed to be watching over the sacred ground. Wilson had trouble believing what he was seeing, because seeing spirits is a Native American thing and he wasn't Native American.

He didn't visit the site as much as some other family members after that. Seeing the forty was something he went through each time he went to the crash site, and the experience wasn't necessarily comforting—in fact, it was weird, even scary. Each time he took visitors to the crash site, he had to prepare himself for the sight of the spirits, silently watching over the sacred ground.

7

MEMORIAL,

INTERRUPTED

Five years after 9/11, construction of the Pentagon Memorial outside Washington, D.C., was in full swing. By contrast, a construction start date at the Flight 93 site had yet to be determined. *USA Today* described prospects for the Shanksville memorial as "still far from reality."

What was the holdup? Actually, there was a series of roadblocks erected by a series of miscreants—or principled opponents to the memorial, depending on your point of view. All told, the roadblocks would obstruct the progress of the memorial for the next three years.

The first roadblock flowed out of the memorial design itself. When the winning design, "Crescent of Embrace," was unveiled in Washington, D.C., supporters of the memorial hoped that the publicity would spark interest and donations. Instead, it stirred up a swarm of bloggers who protested that the red crescent was an Islamic symbol and that architect Paul Murdoch's crescent pointed to Mecca. This complaint was not exactly news, of course; when it chose the design, the stage II jury knew that someone in Somerset had already left a note complaining of the inadvertent religious symbolism. But no one, probably, foresaw the hornet's nest it would arouse.

Leading the charge was Reverend Ron McRae, the leader of a small fundamentalist congregation near Shanksville who was better known as a street preacher—one of those evangelizers who loudly proselytize on street corners, carrying placards that proclaim things like "Repent," "God Hates You," or "Sodomites Burn in Hell." His preaching outside a gay bar in Jenner Township had earned McRae a reputation a few years earlier. Now he had found a target that was even juicier: an apparent Islamic symbol besmirching a patriotic 9/11 memorial.

"This is a memorial to the terrorists who killed those people, not a memorial to the folks who died there innocently," McRae told the local newspaper. "It's a slap in the face." He added, "They wouldn't dare put up the Ten Commandments or the cross of Christ, but they're going to put up a red crescent. That design should be scrapped, and they should go back and pick another one. We're not going to stand idly by and allow this to happen. This preacher and others are going to be out there letting them know what Christians in this community are thinking."

McRae soon found an ally in one of the Flight 93 family members: Tom Burnett Sr., father of the Tom Burnett who helped lead the passenger revolt. As a member of the stage II jury, Burnett had made a case for the impropriety of the apparent Islamic crescent in Murdoch's design. Although he had gone along with the unanimous vote in favor of the design, he was now having second thoughts. Burnett referred to the crescent as "the Flight 93 mosque" and called on the NPS to dump it. If this design went forward, he didn't want his son's name on it. "It's really revolting to me, this whole thing," he said. "It's an insult to my son and all the others."

Various blogs echoed Burnett: a conspiracy was afoot. No one who knew anything about conspiracy theories should have been surprised. Psychologists who have studied conspiracy thinking tell us that it always emerges in the wake of frightening events, such as 9/11. According to political scientists Joseph Uscinski and Joseph Parent, authors of the book *American Conspiracy Theories*, "researchers have found that inducing anxiety or loss of control triggers respondents to see nonexistent patterns and evoke conspiratorial explanations." Paradoxically, such theories give their adherents a sense of control—at least they know who is to blame. Sometimes the villains are thought to be dark forces from outside the country, but increasingly the enemy is within—typically some agency of the U.S. government. (According to Uscinski and Parent, as many as one-third of Americans believe that the Bush administration was somehow behind the 9/11 attacks.) In the case of Flight 93, the conspiracy was thought to be rooted in that most benign of government agencies, the NPS.

When it came to conspiracy theories, Flight 93 generated some humdingers. And, in the age of the Internet, bloggers had an easy means to broadcast and share their notions. Many bloggers were convinced that Flight 93 had never crashed—that the U.S. government had spirited away the passengers and crew (who were still alive somewhere) in a vast plot to delude the American people. The Islamic crescent theory was easier to sell because people could go online and see the design for themselves—and if you didn't look at it too closely, it did look something like an Islamic crescent. The fact that crescents are common in the history of Western architecture was, apparently, beside the point.

With all the sudden brouhaha, winning designer Paul Murdoch never had much of a chance to savor the thrill of victory. When the *Los Angeles Times* came to interview him, they found "a drained-looking Murdoch" seated at his office desk.

"We wanted to use the crescent of trees to embrace the final resting place of the victims—that was the symbolism," explained the tall, mustachioed Murdoch. The circle was intended to direct visitors to the crash site, not Mecca, he said, and was split by the flight path.

But "given that symbols are the stock-in-trade of memorial designers," the *Times* thought Murdoch "guilty of at least a degree of naivete about his plan's potential for controversy." In any case, it was the *intensity* of the furor that most caught Murdoch off guard. The politics of September 11, he said, had become "so highly charged it's hysterical. I mean that in the true sense of the word. This is hysteria. I feel like I've walked into a war."

If this was war, the conspiracy theorists were on full attack. Congressman Tom Tancredo of Colorado complained to the NPS about the Islamic reference and called for scrapping the design. Harry Beam, a retired Army lieutenant colonel from nearby Johnstown, collected 5,300 signatures opposing the design and presented them at the Flight 93 Advisory Commission's quarterly meeting.

■ ■ ■

Now a potential conspiracy-theorist-in-chief was weighing in on the debate: Alec Rawls, who published a book, *Crescent of Betrayal*, to prove his suspicions that the planned memorial was "a terrorist memorial mosque, centered around a half-mile-wide Mecca-oriented crescent."

The NPS asked several religious iconographic and design experts to review Rawls's claims; none found any validity in them. But even though the NPS brought Rawls to Shanksville, where he met with Murdoch and several members from the competition's juries, he remained unpersuaded. After all, conspiracy theorists view evidence and dialogue as red herrings, and Rawls saw the NPS's due diligence as another cover-up by the U.S. government. "No one will tell the truth," he said. "They just lie and lie and lie."

Almost all of the family members, however, pulled together in defense of the "Circle of Embrace" and against Rawls, Burnett, and the bloggers. "Such hate. I'm shocked," said Sandra Felt about the supposed Islamic symbolism in the design. "Any similarities are inadvertent, not intentional," she remarked. "I live on Crescent Place and it's surrounded by maples that turn red in the fall. Should I move?"

"We suggested the name be changed," jury member Henry Cook recalled. Nevertheless, he added, "I think this particular design spoke more strongly to unity and healing."

In the end, Murdoch revamped his design by filling in the crescent with additional trees, so that the "Crescent of Embrace" became the "Circle of Embrace." The conspiracy theorists were not mollified, but the memorial effort could proceed. Still, the Islamic-memorial accusations had set the NPS back several months.

■ ■ ■

The conspiracy theorists, though a significant nuisance, could not really stop the development of the memorial in its tracks. Now, however, the memorial effort was facing someone who could: Congressman Charles Taylor, chair of the House Interior Appropriations subcommittee, which oversees the NPS budget. Taylor refused to release the $10 million that the 2002 act authorizing the memorial had allocated for land acquisition. For three years he stood against the request. "For Taylor, a large landowner in the mountains of western Carolina, the issue comes down to principle," wrote the *Washington Post*. "The federal government is already the largest landowner in the country, and he believes that no additional tax dollars should go to more land buying for this or any other memorial." Lacking that funding, the NPS could not move ahead with buying the site.

It was a strange stand for Taylor to take, given that he was no enemy of federal money going to pet projects in his own North Carolina district. Citizens Against Government Waste had once referred to Taylor as "Porker of the Month," because he conveniently used public funds for projects such as the $3.8 million park built next door to one 127 of his own companies. Most extravagantly, he advocated for a $600 million highway (fortunately, never built) that would slice through the Great Smoky Mountains National Park. Compared to that, the $10 million for the Flight 93 property was pocket change.

Nevertheless, Taylor stood firm against any funding for the memorial. Finally, in 2006, the families took their concerns to Washington, D.C. In a news conference in front of the U.S. Capitol, they joined Senators Rick Santorum and Arlen Specter and Representative Bill Shuster in imploring members of Congress to override Taylor's objections to the funding.

An author for the *Philadelphia Enquirer* lamented, "Victims' families had to resort to begging outside the very building their relatives probably saved: the U.S. Capitol. It was an outrageous insult to memory."

Taylor refused to meet with the families. Instead, he countered with a statement in which he offered to release the money if the families could come up with half of the projected $60 million price tag for the memorial. (As with most disaster memorial projects, the victims' families were driving the fundraising effort, but so far they had only raised $7.5 million.)

But that week the tide was rapidly turning against Taylor. His refusal to release the funds was making national headlines in the same week that Universal Studios released *United 93* with the generous promise to contribute 10 percent of the ticket sales for the opening weekend to the Families of Flight 93. Back in North Carolina, Taylor faced a tough reelection campaign against a famous former pro football player, and the headlines about his blocking the memorial weren't helping. Finally, other congressmen and even the White House put pressure on Taylor, and at the end of the week he caved in and released the funds—just a little too late to help his electoral prospects back home. When the former football player sailed to victory in the polls, Taylor's days as a Washington power broker were effectively over.

. . .

Despite the roadblocks, the Advisory Commission and its partners plowed ahead, meeting regularly and making slow progress on fundraising. The Mount Everest of roadblocks, however, was now in front of them. It was rooted in the crash site itself—or, more specifically, those who owned the site.

Plans for the memorial called for a 2,231-acre landscaped park—enough land to buffer the memorial from off-site development and to extend from the crash site to Lincoln Highway. Early on, the NPS secured easements on 900 of the acres, but this still left about 1,300 acres, spread out over thirteen different privately owned tracts, to be purchased. The families took the lead on rounding up land for the permanent memorial, which they would then transfer to the NPS.

The two most important parcels were owned by PBS Coal and Svonavec, a local family-owned coal company. Although the PBS parcel was by far the largest, the Svonavec property was particularly crucial because it included the sacred ground where Flight 93 had actually crashed. The temporary memorial also happened to be on Svonavec land.

After the crash, the Svonavec family had been as generous as anyone else in Somerset County. They donated the land where the plane actually hit—approximately six acres—and allowed the temporary memorial to be built on their property. But as the negotiations about actually buying the rest of the property got serious, the Svonavecs began to balk. The sticking point was how much the land was worth—and that, it seemed, was wildly open to interpretation.

Armed with the $1 million that Universal Studios had promised from the ticket sales of *United 93*, the Families of Flight 93 felt prepared to negotiate with Svonovec. The families and the NPS had commissioned three separate appraisals of the Svonavec land and determined that its market value was in the realm of $1,000 to $2,000 per acre—or about $500,000 for all 275 acres. The NPS would eventually offer the Svonavecs $250,000, bolstered by an additional $750,000 from the families.

Mike Svonavec, the secretary/treasurer of Svonavec, thought his land was worth a whole lot more. Patrick White, vice president of the Families of Flight 93 and a Florida attorney specializing in land-development issues, reported that Svonavec told him the land was "worth $50 million, but you can have it for $10 million"—that being the highly publicized figure intended to purchase land for the entire memorial.

In a county where neighborly generosity had been the rule toward the families of Flight 93, the Svonavecs now seemed almost a different species, breathtakingly incongruous in their apparent desire to squeeze every last dollar out of their land.

"It's a very sad day," said Somerset County commissioner Pamela Tokar-Ickes, a member of the Federal Advisory Commission. "I think it's an unreasonable amount of money for one of the landowners." Meanwhile, Svonavec denied asking for $10 million or any other amount for his family's land.

In 2007, the standoff with the Svonavecs went from bad to worse when Mike Svonavec put up a cash-donation box near the temporary memorial to pay, he said, for a private security guard he had hired. The temporary memorial didn't need security, said the NPS. The only misdeeds in the last five years had been a couple cases of vandalism.

The ambassadors were aghast when they discovered the box. "Visitors who want to give money for the permanent memorial are going to be confused," said Glessner. They might have thought that they were donating money to the memorial when it was really going into Svonavec's pocket. It was an easy mistake to make, given that the box bore a drawing of an American flag and the words "Flight 93 National Memorial."

So NPS staffers marched out to the temporary memorial, armed with duct tape and a garbage bag, and sealed the donation box. "It's really sad we have to do this," said the NPS's Joanne Hanley. "But we need to protect the public interest and to be able to tell the story in a dignified manner."

The ungainly fracas made national news, and reporters inundated Svonavec with calls. A photo of the fifty-one-year-old Svonavec sitting at his desk made it all the way to the *New York Times*.

"It is difficult," said Svonavec. "I feel like my family, my business and I have been attacked personally."

But to Patrick White, the donation box was a ruse by Svonovec "to avoid dealing earnestly with the families, the NPS, the county, or anyone." White feared that the box was a signal that Svonavec might try to build his own for-profit memorial and museum on the site. "This will gut the project and kill the memorial," White said.

After the donation-box affair, Svonavec struck back by refusing to renew permission for the temporary memorial on his land. The NPS had no choice but to move "the people's memorial" to a nearby site. Dismantling the heartfelt tributes was emotionally wrenching for staff and volunteers. "There were some tears when we took them down," admitted Barbara Black, who oversaw the process.

• • •

White's worst fears—that the Svonavecs might seek to build their own memorial—appeared to be coming true when Svonavec went looking for backup for his own financial demands. He found it in Randall Bell, a real estate appraiser from California who specialized in the ways in which tragic and terrible events—from landslides to mass killings—affect the value of real estate. Bell's past cases included the townhome where O.J. Simpson's ex-wife and a friend were stabbed to death and the house where six-year-old beauty pageant contestant JonBenét Ramsey was strangled. Appraising such properties had earned Bell the moniker "Master of Disaster."

When Bell rolled into Somerset County, he walked through the fields where Flight 93 had crashed. "There was still a lot of debris and I felt sick to my stomach," he told an interviewer. "I felt so bad for the victims, for their families and for our Nation that came under attack." Nonetheless, he said, "It is my job to address some of the practical issues. Clearly, my role is to be a part of the solution to a negative situation, so I stay focused on that."

And stay focused he did. In dealing with other "stigmatized" properties, Bell had found that their value depended largely on the scope of the tragedy, the sale price of other tainted properties, and the amount of media attention the site had received. Many stigmatized properties lose value, but in the case of Svonavec's land, it seemed that the stigma of the forty murders might actually *increase* its value. Bell proposed that a private, for-profit 9/11 museum with a visitor center and other amenities could be built on the land, bringing the property value to a whopping $23.3 million. He estimated that 230,000 people would visit the site each year, yielding nearly $1.9 million annually.

"It's not an emotional issue. It's an economic reality issue," Bell said. "Somebody reasonable, and justifiably so, could apply much

FIG. 23 New York City firemen donated a cross made of steel from the Twin Towers to the Shanksville fire station. Photo: Chuck Wagner.

higher numbers than I have in this case." Now Svonavec had a seemingly defensible asking price for his land.

■ ■ ■

Even as these delays plagued the national memorial effort out at the crash site, the Shanksville firehouse became the site of a dramatic memorial of its own. A cross made of steel from the World Trade Center and mounted atop a platform shaped like the Pentagon was lowered into place outside the firehouse, linking the events of 9/11 and, not incidentally, highlighting the connection between patriotism and Christianity in the response to the attacks.

The two-ton, fourteen-foot beam, fashioned from the rubble of the north tower, was driven the three hundred miles from New York

City to Shanksville, escorted by a cavalcade of hundreds of firefighters riding motorcycles. Nearly a thousand people attended the dedication ceremony, even though the entire population of Shanksville was only about three hundred. The name of each victim was read aloud as everyone bowed their heads in prayer.

• • •

By 2008, a deadline was looming. If construction was not begun in 2009, the memorial would not be ready for dedication in 2011, the ten-year anniversary of 9/11. (By comparison, the Pentagon Memorial had already been completed and dedicated in 2008.) The NPS knew it would face a firestorm of criticism if it didn't have the memorial plaza completed for a 2011 dedication.

If all the other roadblocks were not enough, a lack of funding nagged the memorial effort. Thirty million dollars in private donations was needed, in addition to federal and state funds, to build the entire memorial. The National Park Foundation, the NPS's fundraising partner, was in charge of fundraising efforts, but compared to the other 9/11 sites, the donations were not rolling in. The crash site's location, far from a major city, was part of the problem.

The original plan had been for construction to begin in 2007, so that the whole complex, including the visitor center, could be completed by 2011. As fundraising continued to lag behind, however, that schedule was replaced with a phased rollout. The new timetable called for building just the core of the memorial—the memorial plaza—by 2011. Other components were to be completed as money became available.

Still, the fact that the NPS did not actually own the site was the greatest obstacle. Lacking deeds to the various properties at the site, the memorial would never be built by the ten-year anniversary.

A breakthrough came in March: PBS Coal, which owned the biggest parcel—about 75 percent of the site, stretching out to Lincoln Highway—sold to the families. Svonavec, however, didn't budge.

There was just one surefire way of getting hold of the Svonavec site: seizing it by eminent domain. This, however, was not possible under current law. When it authorized the Flight 93 memorial, Congress had required that the land be acquired from willing sellers.

To end the stalemate, Pennsylvania senators Arlen Specter and Bob Casey stepped in and pushed through an amendment that allowed the federal government to seize any and all properties if necessary. Now the Department of the Interior had a big stick to use against reluctant sellers.

In December 2008, the Flight 93 families appealed directly to President Bush, asking him, during his final days in office, to direct Interior to use the big stick against Svonavec. With days remaining in his term, President Bush agreed, and the NPS and the families reached an accord with Svonavec in mid-January. Under the agreement, a condemnation suit would be filed in federal court, and the NPS would take ownership of the land, with the court eventually determining how much Svonavec would be paid for it.

Even when President Obama assumed office, however, all the needed parcels were still not in hand. Six owners had yet to sell. The smallest parcel was a six-acre property belonging to a local couple, which included a log cabin that they used for weekend retreats.

In May 2009, Secretary of the Interior Ken Salazar traveled up from Washington and met with the landowners personally. He put them on notice that he'd order seizure of their lands if they didn't agree to sell by June 12.

The threat of condemnation sparked an uproar in Somerset County and within the Flight 93 Advisory Commission itself. The federal government taking people's property away went counter to the conservative ethos of the county, and two prominent locals who were on the Advisory Commission abruptly resigned. One of them, Stonycreek Township supervisor Gregory Walker, said that "a trust that landowners had with the Park Service has quickly eroded away." (Walker was running for reelection in an upcoming primary, which may have influenced his public stance.)

Some of the landowners were surprised at the threat of condemnation. They had always been willing to cooperate, they said. Some complained that the NPS had never actually sat down with them to negotiate. Nonetheless, all the landowners ultimately settled more or less amicably for a collective total of $9.5 million. Secretary Salazar praised them as "good neighbors" and "incidental victims of 9/11."

That November, the NPS finally broke ground. The following summer, construction crews started pouring concrete for the memorial plaza.

• • •

On May 3, 2011, Shanksville resident Jeff Ray came out to the construction site to watch the heavy machinery operators grading the

134

FIG. 24 Wrapped in the American flag, Jeff Ray overlooks the construction of the memorial. Photo: *Johnstown Tribune-Democrat* (Todd Berkey).

site. Ray cut a striking figure that morning: he had wrapped himself in an American flag and carried a makeshift sign that read "I Did Not Forget," written in bright red spray paint on a piece of insulation from his garage.

Ray's visit came at a historic moment. The previous day, U.S. Navy Seals had broken into a secret hideout in Pakistan and killed Osama bin Laden, the mastermind of 9/11. Although Ray was happy that the United States had finally managed to "get even," he admitted that he shed tears at the site that day. "Just thinking of all the lives that were lost here just eats me up," he said.

Just four months and eight days hence, a finished memorial plaza would stand there, forever honoring the memories of those forty dead. There were others besides Ray who did not forget.

8

THE
SHANKSVILLE
REDEMPTION

The two-day dedication of the Flight 93 National Memorial on September 10–11, 2011, got off to a late start. A tropical storm had blown through Pennsylvania the previous day, and the open fields atop the abandoned coal mine were saturated with eight inches of rain, which left a sea of mud and a flooded parking lot on Saturday morning. In the predawn hours, pumps were brought in along with truckloads of gravel to firm up the ground. Cars had begun to line up hours before the dedication, and by 10 A.M., when the gates finally opened, officials were saying there were too many cars to handle. They stretched for more than a mile along Route 30, where vendors sold American flags to visitors stuck in traffic.

Inside the park, traffic was virtually at a standstill, and like many other visitors, we ended up parking illegally on the roadside and walking down Skyline Drive. We rounded a curve, and there, down below in the bowl, was the Memorial Plaza.

"*Is that it?*" asked my wife, Ann. And indeed, from the hill high above the crash site, it was hard to imagine that that black streak across the valley floor was the result of tens of millions of dollars and ten years of work. But it was, and we were here on the tenth anniversary of the crash of Flight 93 with four thousand other Americans to witness its dedication.

It wasn't until we got down to the level of the crash site, passed through the security check-in, and began our long walk down the Memorial Plaza that the intent of this stark, unrelenting line of black concrete became apparent. Nothing but a low, sloping retaining wall (originally intended to be black stone, but budget constraints intervened) separated us from the sacred ground, and perhaps fifty yards away, a large boulder in a scrubby field marked the point where the nose of the 757 had plowed into the earth. For an entire decade only family members had access to the sacred ground, but now I could almost reach out and touch it. The overall effect was solemn, austere, and powerful.

As we walked down the plaza, my earlier doubts—about whether a sleek and sophisticated design by a Beverly Hills architect could

FIG. 26 The Wall of Names features the names of the dead inscribed in white marble. National Park Service.

ever rise to the emotional heights of the temporary memorial—fell away. This was a stark, unforgiving design, but absolutely appropriate to the gravity of the place and to those whose remains are interred there. Still, it would take a few subsequent visits before it dawned on me that this memorial gave me what I'd wanted on my first visit to Shanksville five years earlier—to be able to walk next to the crash site and ponder the meaning of it all.

Paul Murdoch had told me that he had not looked to other memorials for inspiration. But as I walked down the Memorial Plaza, it was hard not to see commonalties with Maya Lin's Vietnam Veterans Memorial: the same long black retaining wall, the complete lack of ornament or interpretation, and the intended focus on the solemn *experience* of walking down the black plaza. The lineage of abstract minimalism in memorial design, whose first and greatest exponent was the Vietnam Veterans Memorial, is clearly a powerful precedent from which subsequent memorial designers divorce themselves with great difficulty.

Murdoch's design diverged from Lin's in at least one important detail: the names of the fallen were carved in white marble, not black marble as in Lin's design. (The morning we arrived, the wall was still cloaked in drapery; two former presidents would unveil it later in the day.) Murdoch felt that, after the experience of walking down the solemn black Memorial Plaza, a visitor should see the forty names celebrated and raised up in contrasting white stone. Importantly, all the names had equal status on the wall, with none standing larger or taller than any other. At one end was a faux-distressed wooden ceremonial gate, which would be opened only for family members and dignitaries who wished to walk on the sacred ground.

138

• • •

Up on Skyline Drive, the temporary memorial was no more. Despite the many emotional ties to "the people's memorial," even Donna Glessner, who had put in so many hours there as an ambassador, felt that it was time for it to go. She had been to Oklahoma City and seen the similar chain-link fence with its thousands of tributes, some of which had been left there for years, becoming frayed and tattered. She didn't want the temporary memorial to linger on until it, too, became grungy. Now, hollowed out in the wall of the Memorial Plaza were niches where people could leave a few tributes and love tokens.

This tasteful display, however, was nothing like the massive array of symbols of patriotism and religious faith at the chain-link fence. A returning visitor from Enola, Pennsylvania, posted on TripAdvisor that he came back to see what the new memorial was like and was "very disappointed. The old memorial . . . where anyone could leave something to pay their respects was awesome to look at. It was simple and it worked. This new memorial is cold and heartless."

Conspicuously absent at the top of the ridge, too, were the huge draglines that had stood as sentinels over the crash site. These had been sold as scrap. Initially, the plan had been to keep them as a dramatic site feature, but the expense of maintaining them in safe condition would have been exorbitant.

The chain motels and fast-food joints that locals had feared had never materialized—at least not yet—at the entrance to the memorial on Lincoln Highway. Another, far more dominant off-site feature had marched onto the horizon: tall, gleaming wind turbines that took advantage of the winds blowing across the high ridges. Looking like metal giants marching across the landscape, these twenty-first-century harbingers of clean energy were, to my eyes, beautiful, but many locals despised them because, unlike coal, they produced energy without providing jobs.

There was no shortage of dignitaries delivering speeches during the first day of the two-day dedication. Former president George W. Bush's eyes were "glittering with emotion," as the *Pittsburgh Post-Gazette* put it, when he described the passenger revolt as the "first counteroffensive in the war on terror." "Americans are alive today," he intoned, "because the passengers and crew of Flight 93 chose to act, and we will be forever be grateful." Bush may have uttered much 139 the same words before, but that didn't stop the crowd of grateful Americans from leaping to their feet in a standing ovation.

Bush was followed by a hoarse-voiced former president Bill Clinton, who likened the actions of the passengers and crew to the three hundred Greek warriors who held off a massive Persian army at the Battle of Thermopylae 2,500 years ago and, in the end, saved their country. Clinton then surprised the audience with an apparently spontaneous announcement. He was "aghast," he said, to learn that morning that $10 million was still needed to build the Flight 93 visitor center, and he and House Speaker John Boehner had agreed on the spot to host a fundraiser in Washington to help the partners raise the remaining funds.

When Vice President Joe Biden took the stage, he made no bones about the military significance of Flight 93 and its direct connection to the War on Terror. Stern-faced throughout his speech, Biden hailed "a new generation of warriors": "The 9/11 Generation, inspired by what happened here, 2.8 million young Americans since 9/11, have joined the United States Armed Forces—thousands giving their lives and tens of thousands being wounded to finish the war that began right here."

A very different take on Flight 93's legacy was offered by U.S. Poet Laureate Robert Pinsky, who spoke not of war or peace but of *memory*.

"A people, any people, is what it remembers," said Pinsky. "For us, the American people, Flight 93—because we remember it—has become a significant part of what we are as a people. However, let's acknowledge, on this communal occasion of memory, that whenever we speak of memory, we're also thinking about forgetting. We can't know what our grandchildren and great-grandchildren will remember. There's always the fear of Lethe, the river of forgetfulness."

Pinsky continued, "No one wanted to remember this event. We didn't want the burden, as well as the honor, of this memory." He then recited two poems, the first about "remembering, whether you want to or not," the second about courage. He read the forty names, and, in front of the stage, two huge bells were tolled after each one. Finally, a bagpiper played "Amazing Grace."

• • •

Families and supporters had come from all over the country for the dedication, and after their speeches they mingled with family members at the Wall of Names. The mood, overall, was euphoric. Gordie Felt, now the president of the Families of Flight 93, said, "I'm thrilled that this sacred ground is protected. . . . I have a place to come to be with my brother."

"The whole day has pretty much been a challenge," an emotional Calvin Wilson said. "It's bittersweet. Remember that for eight years that sacred ground was our private cemetery we came to. But we are very pleased. . . . Getting this recognition is paramount in our lives."

Ilse Homer, whose son, Leroy, was the copilot on Flight 93, felt as if she had actually had a conversation with him while the dignitaries were delivering their speeches. "Mom, this isn't for us, is it?" she thought she'd heard him say. "Of course it's for you," she answered, reflecting on his remarkable humility. But Homer's tender mood abruptly shifted as she recalled the Americans who had been killed serving in Afghanistan and Iraq. "They have exceeded the number of all the victims who died on 9/11," she said through her tears. "Their families all mourn just as much as we do."

• • •

The following morning, Sunday, September 11, the parade of speakers, including Pennsylvania governor Tom Corbett, continued to march across the stage set up for the dedication ceremony. The least articulate but most emotional speaker of the weekend was Wally Miller, the "hick coroner," who choked back tears and freely daubed his eyes with a handkerchief before leading a responsive litany. "Pardon me if I don't look up," he said, donning dark glasses to hide his eyes. "It will go a lot better this way." His voice continued to break as he read a selection of lines to which the audience was supposed to respond, "We will remember them." The response was tepid, but Miller read doggedly through his lines before sitting back down and weeping bitterly into his handkerchief. A different response was elicited when Representative Mark Critz of Johnstown took the microphone and reminded the audience of Miller's compassion for the families.

"Wally Miller is not well known nationally," Critz said. "But I think the families of Flight 93 know who Wally Miller is, and I think we owe him a round of applause." The families rose in a standing ovation.

One of the last speakers that morning was Gordie Felt, who summed up the feelings of many family members by returning to the theme of memory. "This is not an easy morning," said Felt with a deep sigh. "The Flight 93 National Memorial is on its way to completion. The sacred ground is safe and secure so that the final resting place of the Flight 93 passengers and crew will be preserved for generations to come. Roads have been built, tributes collected, oral histories recorded, and thousands of concerned citizens join us as we mark the tenth anniversary of September 11. Yet I can't get past the fact that . . . we lost too much those ten years ago.

"Nothing frightens me more than the phrase, 'Time heals all pain.' Do we really want to be fully healed if the end result involves the complete elimination of the pain that links us to all that we lost that morning?" Felt acknowledged the necessity for family members to move ahead with their lives, yet added, "Let us not allow time to heal all of our pain. Let us never forget the horror of September 11. This site will forever stand as a tribute to forty individuals who, under the most horrific conditions, chose to stand as one and fight. Our painful remembrance honors them and keeps them alive in our hearts."

The speeches ended at noon, and Pastor Robert Way, the Shanksville cleric who had walked out onto the crash site on September 11 ten years earlier, offered a closing prayer. Then, off to the left of the stage, President Obama and First Lady Michelle quietly emerged from the wooden gate next to the Wall of Names. Obama had already visited Ground Zero that morning and would finish at the Pentagon that afternoon; here, he solemnly laid a wreath at the foot of the Wall of Names before mingling with family members. There were chants of "USA!" and "Yes we can!" as they made their way through the crowd.

■ ■ ■

Amid the celebrations, the issue of who the "true heroes" of the passenger revolt were had never gone away. Some family members complained that the Wall of Names gave all of the passengers and crew equal billing, regardless of whether they were thought to have led the passenger revolt.

"Everyone on the flight played a role," said Alice Hoagland. "But they did not play an equal role and the monument doesn't reflect that."

"I don't have a problem with honoring the forty but I do have a problem with people being realistic," said Beverly Burnett, mother of Tom Burnett. "We know my son did not hide in his seat. We heard his voice in the cockpit recorder. . . . I know [other families are] grieving for their loved ones but let's not change the storyline. There were people who were not big and strong like my son Tommy."

The Congressional Gold Medal, when it finally came later that year, did not recognize the special bravery of anyone either. It didn't even recognize the difference between Flight 93 and the other doomed flights. Still, it was significant. The Fallen Heroes of 9/11 bill, which was passed in December by the U.S. Senate and House of Representatives, awarded three Congressional Gold Medals—one for each of the 9/11 sites—to generically honor the civilians, public safety workers, airline passengers, and crew members (in other words, everybody) killed. So, once again, with everyone judged a "fallen hero," what did the word "hero" actually mean? The act to authorize the medals was perhaps most notable for the time it took to pass: ten years and three months after the attacks.

. . .

Out on the Stutzmantown Road, the Flight 93 Memorial Chapel formed no part of the official observances of the dedication. The chapel, which had emerged so early and dramatically, seemed to be faltering even as the national memorial was beginning its life. Father Al's health was the stumbling block, a danger sign given that the chapel's survival totally depended on his energy. Now in his late sixties, Father Al had been diagnosed with cancer of the esophagus, vocal cords, and kidneys. When I visited the chapel the following year, he was stooped and ashen and spoke in a whisper through a tube protruding from his throat. I was amazed that he was in the chapel at all.

He had resigned as president of the board of directors earlier that year, declaring, "It is not possible for me to fulfill the functions I need to do, especially to meet the public." But then he withdrew his resignation. Apparently, he just couldn't let go of his dream—and the dream had burgeoned as the decade wore on. The same year he was diagnosed, he had partnered with a Pittsburgh architect on a proposal to pick up the chapel and move it near the new entrance to the national memorial on Route 30. There, at a cost of $10 million, they would add a six-hundred-seat auditorium, a museum, a gift shop, and conference rooms on a thirty-acre site. The NPS expressed concern that the auditorium would steal the thunder of the national memorial. But no angel along the lines of a Maggie Hardy Magerko stepped forward with the money needed for the project, and it never got off the ground.

The day I visited the chapel, volunteers were removing Father Al's priestly paraphernalia, which I did not take as a good sign. When I asked him what he thought of the completed Flight 93 National Memorial, he politely refused to comment.

Without Father Al's driving energy behind the chapel, its future looked very uncertain. But even if Father Al had kept his health, it was hard to see what purpose the chapel, with its amateur-decorator ambience, had now that the Flight 93 National Memorial was in place. It would have even less purpose when the official visitor center was built and outfitted with professionally designed, informative exhibits.

The side-by-side development of the chapel and the national memorial calls to mind the tortoise and the hare. The chapel came into being with meteoric speed only a year after the crash, but a decade later, it was losing momentum, whereas the slow-to-finish national memorial stands a good chance of surviving as long as there is a United States.

· · ·

I introduced myself to Wally Miller at the memorial dedication and told him I was just beginning the research for a book about the effects of the Flight 93 crash on the people of Somerset County. (The research and writing of this book would take more than three years.) Miller readily agreed to an interview, and on the eve of my next visit to Shanksville, I called to set a time. He said that the demands of his mortuary business were such that I would have to call when I was in town and he would decide ad hoc whether he could meet with me.

When I did call again, he said he had a customer with him. Calls on subsequent visits turned up the same answer, and I realized that Miller was starting to see me as a nuisance. The last time I called, he practically hung up on me. The brush-off stung because when he had overseen the crash site in 2001 and 2002, he had granted hundreds of interviews—had never turned down a request. In time, however, I understood that Miller probably did not want to revisit the burden of grief he had carried for so long. I'd simply come on the scene several years too late.

Miller's wife, Arlene—"Arl"—found the experience of working with the victims' remains and the families so profound that she left her job as a chemist and enrolled at the Pittsburgh School of Mortuary Science to become a funeral director. She was valedictorian of her class, and Wally Miller spoke at the graduation ceremony.

After graduating, she became a partner in the Miller Funeral Home and Crematory. Her first professional job was to perform a hair replacement for a woman who'd died after brain surgery. "I was called to this job," she said. "I knew I had something to give that I didn't know before 9/11."

Others whose careers changed included Barbara Black, who left her position as curator at the Somerset Historical Society to take a job as historian and curator at the NPS headquarters at the crash site, where she heads up the oral history project. She was joined by Donna Glessner and Kathie Shaffer, wife of Terry Shaffer, the Shanksville fire chief. A registered nurse who left a better-paying job to focus on the oral history project, Shaffer has conducted 85 percent of the more than seven hundred interviews that the NPS team has completed since 2005, often traveling to both coasts to interview family members. She always begins with the same question: "Can you tell me how your day began on Sept. 11?"

For Shaffer, an empathetic listener, the emotional impact of the interviews—such as seeing grown men break down in front of her—has been grueling. Even the interviewees can see the effect her job has had on her. Once again, the aftermath of the crash has borne down hardest on the most caring individuals. Still, Shaffer says, "this is probably the most important work of my life, other than being a mother and making sure my children are good citizens and good people."

Two interviews that Shaffer has never succeeded in capturing are those with the scrap cutters Michael Shepley and Lee Purbaugh, the only people who had the awful privilege of actually seeing the plane crash. Though she gently hounded them for months, neither consented to relive those terrible moments.

• • •

Family members—widows, for example—have varied widely in their ability to move on with their lives.

Sandy Dahl didn't attend the memorial dedication. Somehow, returning to Shanksville couldn't bring that elusive closure, couldn't assuage the memories of her lost love that still haunted her. "Normally, people have a memorial, and it's behind them then," she told the *Denver Post*. "This is never going away."

Nine years earlier, on the first anniversary of the crash, Dahl had gone to Shanksville and spoken of hope—"hope that carries us through tomorrow when the clouds will part and the sun will shine on our lives again." But for Dahl, the clouds never parted. She continued to wander through the shades of grief and memory, yearning to turn back the clock to the days when she was the wife of the most gallant and romantic airline pilot in the world.

So the dedication of the memorial came and went, and the following May, Sandy Dahl died in her sleep of heart failure while staying at a friend's house. An autopsy revealed an overdose of alcohol, painkillers, and medications for depression and anxiety. Though her death was thought to be an accident, the opiates that had kept her grief at bay had finally caught up with her. She was only fifty-two. The Captain Jason Dahl Scholarship Fund, which she founded, still awards scholarships to aspiring pilots.

By contrast, Dorothy Garcia, the widow of Sonny Garcia, was exemplary in the way she pulled her life back together. Of her involvement in the memorial, specifically her service on the stage II jury, she told me, "Absolutely it was healing. It was something that I could do to honor my husband." Five years after the tragedy, she remarried. A devout Christian, she gave credit to God for restoring her. She has spoken at many churches about her faith and day-to-day recovery. "Every little thing that you do, if you want it to be a positive, it becomes a positive," she said. She desires to write a book about her journey.

Sandra Felt, widow of Edward Felt, has focused on raising their two daughters. They are "healthy and really smart and witty young women," she told me. One is working on an advanced degree, and the other is already established in a career. Felt herself is "learning to laugh again and enjoy and make new memories."

But when I mentioned the notion that working on a memorial—perhaps serving on the stage II jury—might be a healing experience, Felt stopped me short. "Whoever said that didn't know what the hell they were talking about," she said. "Try ripping an old scar open and what do you get? A deeper scar. But I must be a sucker for pain because I kept doing it."

Her brother-in-law, Gordie Felt, has had a different experience. "My involvement," he told me, "has allowed me to channel the anger and rage that easily could have consumed me into a productive effort to honor those lost on Flight 93."

Father Al died in hospice on February 15, 2013. Despite his excommunication, Saint Peter's Roman Catholic Church in Somerset laid him to rest with a funeral Mass. Wally Miller handled the funeral arrangements.

Looking back on Father Al's journey, it would be easy to see him as a figure of pity, a manic-depressive who was defrocked by his own church. In his work at the chapel, however, he found the greatest fulfillment he had ever known. That personal mission was so drenched in meaning that he willingly bent his whole life to its service. In what others might see as a sad obsession, I suspect he found his soul's own peace.

· · ·

In December 2013, U.S. District Judge Donetta Ambrose in Pittsburgh determined the value of the Svonavecs' 275 acres to be $1,535,000, based on the findings of an expert eminent-domain commission that she appointed.

Michael Svonavec's response was to sue the government for allegedly lowballing him. He was still seeking the $23 million he said he could have earned had he built a museum on the crash site and charged admission. Indeed, visitation swelled after the permanent memorial was in place, proving that a growing public did want to view the crash site. The NPS reported that the memorial received nearly 350,000 visitors in 2012, the first full year it was open following its dedication.

· · ·

Visitors who came to the site after the dedication would all be predisposed to reverence due to what had happened there. The actual *design* of the Memorial Plaza would, however, receive mixed reviews. In the four years between the dedication of the Memorial Plaza and the construction of the visitor center, some commented on TripAdvisor that the memorial was "unfinished," even "temporary." It was as if the Memorial Plaza—that stark line of black concrete alongside the sacred ground—was somehow not the "real" memorial. Representative comments included "Hallowed but lacking"; "Still in the works and I know many have been disappointed"; "Beautiful views of nature but the temporary memorial is anticlimactic"; and "Appears to be shaping up nicely but right now it is very stark."

Other visitors, however, thought that the minimalist design of the Memorial Plaza was just right. "In my humble opinion," one woman posted, "the memorial site does not need expanding, as what has been done already is fitting and appropriate; the large visitor complex being built overlooking the crash site will inevitably be impressive, but is it really needed? I can see the need to raise awareness and educate, but I think that can be achieved with what is already there."

Comparisons with the chain-link "people's memorial" simply would not go away. Chuck Wagner, who served as ambassador at the temporary memorial for years and has continued to serve at the Memorial Plaza, can't help but notice the difference in visitors' reactions. Of the temporary memorial, he told me, "A lot of tears were shed there. You don't see much of that anymore—not the heartfelt connection that there used to be."

Of course, the waters of Lethe, the river of forgetfulness, have flowed on since 9/11, and the memory of that traumatic day may be losing its power to draw forth tears. This sparks another question: As other mass tragedies come and go in this country, will the blank-slate wall of the Memorial Plaza have anything to say to future visitors who ask ever-changing questions? "Memorials, being fixed in concrete and stone, have an inherent problem because memories aren't fixed," wrote *New York Times* critic Michael Kimmelman.

So is a memorial that seems to say nothing at all a memorial that will speak to the future? Kimmelman thinks it is. "Minimalist abstraction, with its allegorical pliancy, turns out to function in a memorial context as the best available mirror for a modern world aware of its own constantly changing sense of history."

• • •

And what of the sweet village of Shanksville? With the dignitaries and the television cameras long gone, would Shanksville return to its family-oriented lifestyle, its neighborly generosity, and the friendliness of its front porch–lined streets?

Disaster scholar Ed Linenthal posited that healthy communities cannot be built on piles of dead bodies. But as I walk down Shanksville's quiet streets today, there are no outward scars to be seen, and the locals I have talked to, while conscious of the burden that history and memory have laid upon them, seem to be shouldering that burden gracefully.

Visible changes to Shanksville include the American flags that fly up and down Main Street and throughout the village, along with street signs that display a flag theme—legacies of the patriotic fervor that followed 9/11. The local school features a rock garden adorned with a memorial sculpture. And, of course, there is the massive cross at the Shanksville firehouse.

Tourist traffic to the memorial has been diverted away from Shanksville, which means that the little village has lapsed back into the gentle solitude of former decades. This also means, however, that any economic windfall from tourist dollars will never flow to Shanksville, never lift it out of its economic stagnation. Travelers, should they choose to pass through Shanksville, still can't gas up their car in the village or spend a night there, because it hasn't built a filling station or even the tiniest of motels.

"Shanksville's roads are too small, and the water system is not up to the expansion," says Jerry Spangler. "The economic rewards [of the new memorial] are not going to be reaped by the community."

• • •

Not everybody around Shanksville was thrilled with the new memorial. Ernie Stotler, a retired school counselor who lives near the boundary of the park, told me that he had four brothers and a sister who lived within five miles of it but hadn't attended the dedication and were surprised that he had. In this conservative, salt-of-the-earth county where natives are not given to pomp and spectacle, some felt it was all overdone.

Other locals saw the memorial quite differently.

One frigid day in December following the dedication, a blue pickup truck bearing the brightly painted words "Let's Roll" drove down the snow-covered hillside toward the Memorial Plaza. When it came to rest in the parking lot, Terry Butler stepped out and walked out along the plaza, an envelope in his hand. He bent to leave it in one of the receptacles hollowed out of the wall for tributes. It was a Christmas card addressed to the heroes of Flight 93, a remembrance of what they had done for his country—the sacrifice to whose memory he had consecrated his life. He had left a card like this one at the temporary memorial every Christmas since 9/11, and now he left one at the black Memorial Plaza that stretched out under the December sky. But it was too cold to linger in this place, and Butler walked back to his truck and drove away across the vast, snowy landscape.

Acknowledgments

The genesis of this book was a call to Jeff Reinbold, the project manager of the Flight 93 Memorial, in the summer of 2011. I had learned that the memorial was under construction, and during our conversation Jeff said he thought there was the makings of a book in the ten-year evolution of the project. He invited me to visit the National Park Service headquarters on the old strip mine where Flight 93 had crashed almost ten years earlier. So began a process of research and writing that would stretch out to four years and many visits to the crash site.

When I and my wife, Ann, first drove from our home in Washington, D.C., to the high plateau where Flight 93 crashed, Warren Byrd, the landscape architect of the project, was there to give me a tour of the almost-complete national memorial. Although I had visited the temporary memorial built by local people overlooking the crash site a few years earlier, walking down the recently poured black-concrete memorial plaza was a completely different experience. For one thing, the plaza butted right up against the "sacred ground" where Flight 93 had plowed into the earth. Being that close to "ground zero" of the crash was moving in itself.

Many subsequent visits to the memorial were spent at the onsite National Park Service (NPS) headquarters. There, Ann and I sat at a small table and read through hundreds of oral histories—face-to-face interviews with first responders, family members, Shanksville residents, and many others—that the NPS had initiated and compiled. Through reading them and meeting with people around Shanksville, Ann had the insight that the aftermath of Flight 93 was really a love story—a sad but sustaining love between the good people of

Shanksville and the bereaved families of Flight 93. I hope I have conveyed some of that love in the early chapters of this book.

The oral histories became the primary source material for the book, and for them I am very grateful to the NPS team, beginning with Barbara Black, who initiated the oral history project and was unfailingly generous in granting me access to the histories. Kathie Shaffer, who had personally conducted most of the hundreds of interviews, was always most kind in organizing them for our visits and advising me on which histories best suited my research interests. Donna Glessner gave me an illuminating tour of Shanksville from the perspective of someone whose family had lived there for generations. She also searched through NPS files to provide essential documentary photographs and maps.

My gratitude goes out to others who contributed to my research effort, starting with memorial scholar Ed Linenthal, who offered his expert advice on disaster research and a list of suggested readings that deepened my understanding of memorials and the issues that swirl around them. The book that most opened my eyes was *Memorial Mania* by Erika Doss.

My thanks to John Reynolds, chair of the Flight 93 Advisory Commission, for warmly introducing me to the commission, thereby lending me credibility and opening the door to interviews with members of the Families of Flight 93. Jerry Spangler of the Advisory Commission lent me the important *Flight 93 Advisory Commission Briefing Book* and later reviewed chapter 7 of my manuscript before publication. Tim Baird of the Penn State Department of Landscape Architecture provided background on the design competition that he was instrumental in organizing and gave me a copy of the competition brief. Shanksville resident Chuck Wagner generously provided photographs of Shanksville and the Flight 93 site, and Chip Minemeyer, editor of the *Johnstown Tribune-Democrat* allowed me to use photographs of key individuals in the book.

My thanks to those who were key to the editing process, beginning with Kathryn Yahner, my editor at Penn State University Press, for believing in this project and for her sound editorial advice and patience in seeing it through to completion. Pennsylvania author Mark Harris kindly gave advice and encouragement early on. Former Smithsonian magazine editor Helen Starkweather gave me professional advice on an early draft of the text. My colleague Linda McIntyre lent much-needed encouragement.

A very special thanks to my friend, landscape architect and writer Kim Sorvig, who read and edited early drafts of the entire text, often calling for sweeping changes that, as it turned out, improved the manuscript. Without Kim's help and guidance, this would be a very different (and lesser) book.

Finally, this book is a tribute to the support and encouragement of my wife, Ann. She was by my side on umpteen trips to Shanksville and served as what she jokingly referred to as my "editorial assistant" in plowing through those hundreds of oral histories. Without her unflagging help and optimism over a four-year period, this book would never have seen the light of day.

Appendix: The Memorial Design Competition Juries

M. Paul Friedberg, landscape architect, New York
Donna Graves, arts planning consultant, Berkeley, Calif.
Richard Haag, landscape architect, Seattle
David Hollenberg, National Park Service, Philadelphia
Carole O'Hare, family member, Danville, Calif.
Michael Rotondi, architect and educator, Los Angeles
Cecil Steward, College of Architecture, University of Nebraska
Susan Szenasy, editor in chief, *Metropolis Magazine*

Julie Bargmann, University of Virginia
Gerald Bingham, family member, Wildwood, Fla.
Thomas E. Burnett Sr., family member, Northfield, Minn.
Robert Campbell, architecture critic, *Boston Globe*
Barbara Catuzzi, family member, Houston
G. Henry Cook, president and CEO, Somerset Trust Company
Gail Dubrow, University of Minnesota
Sandra Felt, family member, Matawan, N.J.
Charles Fox, Somerset Historical Center
Dorothy Garcia, family member, Portola Valley, Calif.
Ilsa Homer, family member, Hauppauge, N.Y.
Connie Hummel, principal, Shanksville High School
Jonathan Jarvis, National Park Service, Oakland, Calif.
Laurie Olin, landscape architect, Philadelphia
Edwin Root, family member, Coopersburg, Pa.
Thomas Sokolowski, Andy Warhol Museum, Pittsburgh
Paula Nacke Jacobs, family member, Baltimore (nonvoting recorder)

Helene Fried, Helene Fried Associates, Oakland, Calif.
Donald J. Stastny, StastnyBrun Architects, Portland, Ore.

Timothy Baird, Flight 93 Memorial Task Force, Department of Landscape
    Architecture, Pennsylvania State University
Gina Bradshaw Farfour, Families of Flight 93 Board, Banner Elk, N.C.
Jeffrey Reinbold, National Park Service, Shanksville, Pa.
Calvin E. Wilson, Flight 93 Advisory Commission, Fairfax, Va.

Notes

CHAPTER 1

1   *It was a beautiful morning:* Robyn Blanset and Ray Stevens, OH 41,
    5–9.
2   *At the Somerset barracks:* Kashurba, *Quiet Courage,* 20.
    Terry Butler was taking a radiator out: Ibid., 9–10.
    Linda Shepley was going out to hang clothes: Linda Shepley, OH 53, 3.
3   *At the Rollock scrap yard:* Timothy Lensbouer, OH 297, 4–7.
    When they threw open the door: Nena Lensbouer, OH 260, 5–9.
4   *Two and a half miles away:* Kashurba, *Quiet Courage,* 16–17.
6   *At that very moment, two other firemen:* Norbert Rosenbaum, OH
    160, 6–7.
    It didn't take long for paramedic Christian Boyd: Christian Boyd, OH
    25, 26.
7   *Christian came upon a Bible:* Ibid., 18.
    *Mike Sube was still searching / Roger Bailey, also with the county fire
    department:* Kashurba, *Quiet Courage,* 33, 35.
    Louis Veitz, an accident reconstruction specialist: Louis Veitz, OH
    105, 16.
8   *As reporter Jon Meyer was leaving:* Kashurba, *Quiet Courage,* 43–44.
    Photojournalist Sean Stipp got the call: Sean Stipp, OH 111, 43.
    County coroner Wally Miller drove: Perl, "Hallowed Ground."
9   *Miller sensed not people:* Wright, "On Hallowed Ground."
    The first thing Robyn Blanset heard: Robyn Blanset and Ray Stevens,
    OH 41, 12.
    As Shanksville pastor Robert Way drove: Robert Way, OH 52, 9–11.
10 *At Stoystown Auto Wreckers:* Terry Butler, personal interview, April
    2014.
    Jason Fedok watched coroner Wally Miller: Jason Fedok, OH 55,
    19–20.

11 *But he did know people across the state / In the early afternoon, Miller was called:* Wallace Miller, OH 305, 14–19, 29–31.

12 *Almost constant phone calls:* Kashurba, *Quiet Courage*, 38.

13 *Photographer Sean Stipp's biggest impression:* Sean Stipp, OH 111, 45. *Families were devastated:* Lori Guadagno, OH 196, 32–38.

14 *Erich Bay and his wife:* Erich Bay, OH 15, 10–12.

15 *In Denver, Sandra Dahl:* Sandra Dahl, OH 173, 6–12.

16 *Early in the morning in suburban San Diego:* Deborah Borza, OH 11, 11–23.

17 *"None of us will ever forget":* Kashurba, *Quiet Courage*, 84. *First responder Norbert Rosenbaum:* Norbert Rosenbaum, OH 160, 19.

18 *Night descended on the site / Terry Butler, the auto wrecker:* Kashurba, *Quiet Courage*, 81–82. *Wally Miller didn't leave for home:* Arlene Miller, OH 484, 12–13.

CHAPTER 2

20 *In 1798 a German named Christian Shank:* Brett, *Reflections of Stonycreek*, 7–8.

21 *Shanksville's Memorial Day parade:* Ibid.

22 *A farmer would follow a seam:* Ibid., 52. *Still, the village remained a tiny borough:* Ibid., 65.

23 *Coal mining outside the village:* Ibid., 53–54. *That left only one employment center:* Donna Glessner, personal interview, April 2013. *The village "has a heartbeat":* Chuck Wagner, personal interview, July 2014.

24 *"We kind of were not even a spot on the map":* Severson, "Shanksville One Year Later." *Clay Mankmeyer, a retired state trooper:* Lovering, "Sept. 11 Crash Spared." *John Murtha, U.S. representative from Johnstown:* Bosak, "Transcripts Boost Claim," 26.

25 *"I believe they fought and dove":* Ibid.

26 *"We're not—at least I'm not—versed in world events":* Severson, "Shanksville One Year Later." *Kim Friedline stenciled the first sign:* Judi Baeckel, OH 21, 9–11. *By the beginning of the twenty-first century:* Doss, *Memorial Mania*, 69.

27 *according to American studies scholar Erika Doss:* Ibid., 71. *state trooper Terry Wilson climbed:* Kashurba, *Quiet Courage*, 87.

27 *Because the crash site was clearly the scene of a crime:* "Response and
    Recovery"; "Frequently Asked Questions—Flight 93 and Sep-
    tember 11."

28 *Combing the ground around the crater:* Kashurba, *Quiet Courage*, 112.
    As accident reconstruction specialist Louis Veitz: Louis Veitz, OH 105,
    19.
    Arborists Mark Trautman and Ben Haupt: Mark Trautman, OH 163,
    13–17.

29 *In charge of the DMORT morgue operation:* Paul Sledzik, personal
    interview, September 2013.
    The single goal of the DMORT team: Paul Sledzik, OH 475, 37–42.
    State trooper James Broderick was working security: James Broderick,
    OH 6, 26–29.

30 *Sledzik felt a need to reach out:* Paul Sledzik, personal interview,
    September 2013.
    Meanwhile, the FBI had hired local excavators: "Frequently Asked
    Questions—Flight 93 and September 11"; Chuck Wagner, per-
    sonal interview, July 2014.

31 *On Saturday, the U.S. senators from Pennsylvania:* O'Toole and Lash,
    "Prayers Memorialize Flight 93 Victims."

32 *"I want to send a message to our enemy":* Weisberg, "Huge Flag Will
    Be Unfurled."
    It got so that when Pastor Way: Robert Way, OH 52, 31–32; Kashur-
    ba, *Quiet Courage*, 98–99.
    Pastor Way delivered a sermon: Robert Way, OH 52, 27–32.
    Pastor Ed DeVore in nearby Friedens: Kashurba, *Quiet Courage*, 99.

33 *In Oklahoma City, where a daycare center:* Linenthal, *Unfinished
    Bombing*, 119–20.
    And at least one commentator felt: Doss, *Memorial Mania*, 155.
    So they built an impromptu memorial: Kashurba, *Quiet Courage*, 137.
    Pennsylvania Lieutenant Governor Mark Schweiker: Gibb, "Stoic
    Father Visits Somerset Crash Site."

34 *Even hardened reporters were affected:* Kashurba, *Quiet Courage*,
    251–53.
    On the Monday following the crash: Haddock, "Heroes of Flight 93
    Honored."
    At Seven Springs Mountain Resort: Gordon Felt, OH 245, 14.
    Wally Miller came over and met: Wallace Miller, OH 305, 23.

35 *For Barbara Catuzzi:* Barbara Catuzzi, OH 188, 36–37.
    Allison Vadhan of Atlantic Beach: Allison Vadhan, OH 417, 26–27.
    One of them was Judi Baeckel / Then the locals unfurled: Judi Baeckel,
    OH 21, 32–33.

36 *One of them was Frank Monaco:* Frank Monaco, OH 82, 32–33.
37 *As the families stepped down:* O'Toole, Fuoco, and Gibb, "First Lady Meets Flight 93 Families."
      Glenn Kashurba, a Somerset psychiatrist: Kashurba, *Quiet Courage*, 154–55.
      It was hard for Frank Monaco: Frank Monaco, OH 82, 34.
      Allison Vadhan, who hadn't wanted to come: Allison Vadhan, OH 417, 26–27.
      Jack Grandcolas of California: Jack Grandcolas, OH 12, 52.
38 *The families lingered / Bush later told reporters:* O'Toole, Fuoco, and Gibb, "First Lady Meets Flight 93 Families."
      Gordie Felt stepped forward: Gordon Felt, OH 245, 15–16.
39 *Vernon Spangler, the farmer who used to own:* Gibb, "Flight 93 Crash Site Touted."
      Cultural geographer Kenneth Foote: Foote, *Shadowed Ground*, 8–28.
40 *Yet the community of Oklahoma City came together:* Oklahoma City National Memorial and Museum.
      The University of Texas, for instance: "U. Texas's Tower Garden Memorial."
      FBI agent Todd McCall: Todd McCall, OH 687, 72–73.

CHAPTER 3

42 *On September 20, 2001:* "President Bush Addresses the Nation."
43 *According to Cynthia Weber:* Weber, "Popular Visual Language," S141–S142.
      Hers was to be a very public grief: Duryea, "Keeping Us Rolling"; Perry, "Marketing of Lisa Beamer."
      Some Flight 93 family members: Longman, *Among the Heroes*, 244.
44 *"September 11's forgotten flight" / "Here, the best pictures":* Perl, "Hallowed Ground."
      The county government wasn't sure / Black had never dealt: Kashurba, *Quiet Courage*, 201–2.
45 *Congressman Murtha from Johnstown stepped in:* Jeff Reinbold, personal interview, July 2014.
      Wally Miller made a grim calculation: Wright, "On Hallowed Ground."
      By now the "hick coroner": Mayer and Faher, "Flight 93 Coroner," C3.
46 *"That's not what I do":* Dennis Dirkmaat, OH 446, 44.
      So Miller made it his mission: Perl, "Hallowed Ground."
      "I wanted to get the mindset": Faher, "Just the Right Person," 199.

47 *Even when superstar news anchor Katie Couric:* Jack Grandcolas, OH 12, 54.

"He's tired, very tired": Gibb, "Newsmaker."

One night he got a call at 4 A.M.: Hamill, "Seven Years Later."

Gordie Felt found it "overwhelming": Kashurba, *Quiet Courage*, 182.

Grace Sherwood, the daughter of Jean Peterson: Grace Sherwood, OH 479, 54.

48 *Gordie Felt found it amazing:* Kashurba, *Quiet Courage*, 182.

When Ben Wainio, father of Honor Elizabeth: Zaslow, "Plans to Honor Sept. 11 'Heroes.'"

Lyz Glick, the wife of Jeremy Glick: Lyzbeth Glick Best, OH 338, 52.

Just nine days after the flight: Last, "Precious Medals."

49 *The bill's main sponsor / "Honor everybody or nobody" / "They were all heroes" / Senator Arlen Specter:* Zaslow, "Plans to Honor Sept. 11 'Heroes.'"

"Someone who voluntarily leaves" / U.S. Airways captain Chesley Sullenberger: Weeks, "Heroic Acts."

50 *One FBI agent who worked at the crash site:* Longman, *Among the Heroes*, 263.

the "polite fiction" / "I think it's a beautiful story": Lamb, "Flight 93 Families Divided."

51 *A modern myth, by a better definition:* Chernus, "Meaning of 'Myth.'"

Dale Nacke, the brother of Louis Nacke: Dale Nacke, OH 191, 37.

"I don't think Mom and Don were up there fighting": Grace Sherwood, OH 479, 40.

52 *"Every era, every culture deals with grief":* Tippett, "Dario Robleto."

the memorialist's main way of honoring: Berger, *Five Ways We Grieve*, 56.

A prime example of a memorialist: Sandra Bodley, OH 289, 3–4; Nancy Mangum-Bodley, OH 288, 15–16.

Berger found that memorialists / Berger found that the more closely: Berger, *Five Ways We Grieve*, 58.

CHAPTER 4

54 *It was a bitterly cold December afternoon:* Edward Linenthal, OH 747, 12–14.

56 *"Why do we make memorials":* Doss, *Memorial Mania*, 1–2.

"The inevitability of forgetting": Hariman and Lucaites, "Vernacular Memorials and Civic Decline," 129.

On the cold December evening of the town meeting: "Flight 93 Public Meeting," 28–30.

Notes

57 *Joanne Hanley, superintendent of the national parks:* Hanley, *Thoughts on Next Steps,* n.p.
  Janet Coughenour rose to the microphone: "Flight 93 Public Meeting," 32–33.
  Robert Leverknight from nearby Lambertsville: Ibid., 17–18.
58 *A state representative in Pennsylvania:* Ibid., 52–53.
  Then Phil Thompson was introduced: Ibid., 51–61.
59 *He was not your average country priest:* Hamill, "Flight 93 Memorial Chapel's New Vision."
  the passengers "prayed together": Alphonse Mascherino, OH 347, 30.
60 *Around Christmas he had a dream:* Ibid., 36–39.
61 *One of them was Derrill Bodley:* Reitman, "Afghan Journey."
  Not all the Flight 93 families: Nancy Mangum-Bodley, OH 288, 20, 22, 25.
  It was a trip Bodley almost didn't make / Bodley returned: Reitman, "Afghan Journey."
62 *Local curator Barbara Black:* Kashurba, *Quiet Courage,* 206–7.
  "At first, it wasn't the story": Zaslow, "Near Shanksville, Pa."
  One day, Esther Heymann: Yates, "Pa. Locals, Flight 93 Families United."
63 *Such empathy for family members / Some ambassadors undertook:* Zaslow, "Near Shanksville, Pa."
65 *"This ain't Disneyland":* Clines, "Threats and Responses."
  Donna Glessner got used to sights: Donna Glessner, personal interview, April 2013.
  A family from Louisiana: Schuler, "Pilgrimage to Shanksville," 2–4.
66 *Rhoda Schuler, a theology student from Minnesota:* Ibid., 4–7.
  the forty heroes provided "a glimpse": Ibid., 37.
  as Ed Linenthal would point out: Perl, "Hallowed Ground."
67 *As the remains were returned to the families:* Ibid.
  "Well, they're going to have to handle it": Arlene Miller, OH 484, 27.
  Miller broke down: Ibid., 35.
68 *"You see all that wire":* Faher, "Just the Right Person," 199.
  Anyway, Miller wasn't sold on the idea / At the Somerset Alliance Church: Perl, "Hallowed Ground."
  "I don't care about fame and notoriety": Ruggieri, "Reflections on a Day," 117.
69 *Donna Glessner and the Flight 93 ambassadors:* Zaslow, "Near Shanksville, Pa."
  "Imagine a school assignment": Hariman and Lucaites, "Vernacular Memorials and Civic Decline," 127.

69 *Barbara Black, however, did not discriminate:* Griffith, "This Is to Remind Us," 175.

   "We are not making judgments": Levine, "Honoring Lives Lost."

   In California, Deena Burnett: Quinn, "Widow Presses FBI."

70 *"I can't see how hearing" / The FBI warned:* Levin, "Flight 93 Families Hear Cockpit Tape."

   "I expect my husband's voice": Quinn, "Widow Presses FBI."

   Sandy Dahl, however, was convinced: "Flight 93 Pilot's Wife."

71 *At one point in the thirty-minute tape:* Coile and Lee, "Flight 93 Relatives Listen."

   escorted family members to their cars / "I wish there was a video": Levin, "Flight 93 Families Hear Cockpit Tape."

   the Shanksville High School graduation ceremony: Rock, "Giuliani Tells Shanksville Students," 1.

72 *"This is a happy day and that's a sad thing":* Ibid., 2.

   It included appropriations: Hefling, "N.C. Congressman Blocks."

   Back in Shanksville, Father Al: Alphonse Mascherino, OH 347, 41–42.

73 *"Either you go or the chapel goes":* Ibid., 51.

74 *"The chapel is my expression":* Ibid., 49.

   One day Wally Miller: Wallace Miller, OH 305, 65–66.

   On the first anniversary of the crash: "'America Is Grateful.'"

75 *Sandy Dahl, who was fast becoming a spokesperson:* Powell, "Shanksville, Pennsylvania."

   A strong subtext of the ceremony / "Today, we also honor and thank": Ibid.

76 *Shortly after noon, President Bush arrived / A somewhat different note:* "'America Is Grateful.'"

CHAPTER 5

77 *One minute before the five o'clock deadline:* Schrock, "Down to the Wire."

78 *"It had to be [open]," said Carole O'Hare:* Fraser, "Sacred Ground," 26.

   The operational arm of the partners: Flight 93 National Memorial newsletter, no. 1.

79 *"There was an awkward situation":* Jerry Spangler, personal interview, April 2014.

   "honor the heroes of Flight 93": Competition briefing book, 4.

   This reflected the Oklahoma City model: "Flight 93 Public Meeting," Flight 93 Advisory Commission Briefing Book, 51–61.

The slow progress in reaching a consensus: Flight 93 National Memorial newsletter, no. 2; "Flight 93 National Memorial Mission Statement."

Working with the NPS: Flight 93 National Memorial newsletter, no. 2.

80 *This whopping acreage / "to see the 'battlefield'":* First, "Eminent Domain Only Way."

But acquiring so much real estate: Fehrman, "Forgotten Memorial."

Opening the boxes had been an event: Don Stastny, personal interview, March 2014.

82 *"And here's the beauty of it":* Freyvogel, "Flight 93 Memorial Designs Revealed," 1B.

84 *It reached its ultimate expression:* Doss, *Memorial Mania*, 125–26.

It is the second most visited memorial: Annual Park Ranking Report.

86 *A headline in the "Baltimore Sun":* Baltimore Sun, June 22, 1997.

It ranks third in visitation: Annual Park Ranking Report.

87 *They even went so far as to fire:* Linenthal, *Unfinished Bombing*, 187.

"The emotional component": Sandra Felt, personal interview, January 2014.

The jury comprised / The stage I jury's task: "International Design Competition."

"It's incredible to me": Reed Ward, "Panel Narrows Entries."

The next morning: "International Design Competition."

88 *On the final day:* Ibid.

The youngest finalist: Chruscicki, *CBC Nightly News* coverage.

91 *At the other end of the professional spectrum:* Paul Murdoch, personal interview, June 2015.

95 *Another very established finalist:* Steiner, *Design for a Vulnerable Planet*, 222–27.

97 *Finalists Leor and Gilat Lovinger:* Leor Lovinger, personal correspondence.

98 *The only finalist who lived within driving distance:* Laurel McSherry, personal interview, August 2015.

101 *"Above all other entries":* Lowry, "Analysis."

The stage II jury, which had the monumental burden: Stage II Jury Report.

Sandra Felt, the wife of Flight 93 passenger Edward Felt: Sandra Felt, personal interview, January 2013.

102 *Henry Cook, president of the Somerset Trust Company:* Henry Cook, personal interview, August 2013.

Like the stage I jury: Stage II Jury Report.

103 *Some of their comments / In the first two days:* Ibid.

104 *"It looks like a diet meal":* Henry Cook, personal interview, August
2013.

For Sandra Felt, however: Sandra Felt, personal interview, January
2013.

Calvin Wilson, who was present: Calvin Wilson, OH 185, 4.

105 *"['Crescent of Embrace'] best addresses":* Stage II Jury Report.

A local preacher had noticed this: Don Stastny, personal interview,
March 2014.

"Consider the interpretation and impact": Stage II Jury Report.

Murdoch's evaluation of the temporary memorial: Thoren, "Flight 93,"
66.

Ed Klein, a Shanksville ambassador: Zaslow, "Near Shanksville, Pa."

106 *"We don't need giant statues":* Lileks, "Sorry State."

"The Hallmark-card Minimalism" / *"too reflective":* Hawthorne,
"Reading Symbolism."

"Optimistically," said Hamilton Peterson: Forgey, "Flight 93 Memorial Design Unveiled."

CHAPTER 6

107 *In a small Amish community:* Kraybill, Nolt, and Weaver-Zercher,
Amish Grace, 17–29.

108 *In the same year, three hundred miles south:* Hauser and O'Connor,
"Virginia Tech Shooting."

"I hope that if I ever meet anyone like you": Hauser, "Virginia Tech
Sets Out."

109 *The Virginia Tech massacre sparked:* Somashekhar, "Memories of
Va. Tech."

people with a history of mental instability: "Seung-Hui Cho Biography."

110 *Paul Greengrass, who wrote and directed* / *Family members clashed:*
Longman, "Paul Greengrass's Filming."

111 *"The jury's still out":* Coomarasamy, "9/11 Film Premiere Ignites
Debate."

Film critic Bob Mondello: Mondello, "'United 93.'"

In the end, "United 93": Toumarkine, "United 93."

On hand to greet every visitor / *"Probably the worst fate":* Alphonse
Mascherino, OH 347, 81.

112 *"I don't have any life to speak of":* Ibid., 84.

113 *On September 11, 2006:* Lester, "Chapel Pays Homage."

114 *Bishop Adamec, who had previously warned* / *Trying to put the best
spin:* Hamill, "Flight 93 Memorial Chapel's New Vision."

Butler got his first tattoo: Terry Butler, personal interview, April 2014.

116 *A song performed at Father Al's chapel:* Clifton, "Highland Lakes Dancers"; "Prayer for Our Time."

117 *These included a Flight 93 flag:* Kyle, "Pennsylvania Firefighter."

118 *Larry and Barbara Catuzzi looked for ways / Sometimes, on September 11:* Shauk, "Tragedy Victim's Legacy Grows."

119 *They certainly didn't heal Sandy Dahl:* Ingold, "The Wife."

120 *"A lot of people talk about getting closure":* Mayer and Faher, "Flight 93 Coroner," C4.

Ed Linenthal's many interviews / Memory, Linenthal concluded: Edward T. Linenthal, OH 747, 12.

Cathy Stefani, mother of passenger Nicole Miller: Garofoli and Squatriglia, "9/11: Five Years Later."

"Survivor guilt" was a fallout of the crash: Kim Stroka, OH 529, 13–19.

Flying had also become fearful / An odd corollary: Garofoli and Squatriglia, "9/11: Five Years Later."

121 *Derrill Bodley, who had lost his beloved daughter:* Stone, "Derrill Bodley Killed."

Beatrice Guadagno, mother of Richard Guadagno: Beatrice Guadagno, OH 195, 48–49.

One of these was Calvin Wilson: Calvin Wilson, OH 185, 44.

CHAPTER 7

123 *"USA Today" described prospects:* Moore, "For Flight 93 Memorial."

This complaint was not exactly news: Don Stastny, personal interview, March 2014.

124 *Leading the charge / "This is a memorial":* Swauger, "Flight 93 Memorial Challenged."

Although he had gone along: Don Stastny, personal interview, March 2014.

"It's really revolting to me": Hamill, "Design of a Memorial."

Psychologists who have studied conspiracy thinking: Shermer, "Why Do People Believe."

125 *Many bloggers were convinced:* "Flight 93 Never Crashed."

When the "Los Angeles Times" came to interview: Hawthorne, "Reading Symbolism."

Congressman Tom Tancredo: Ibid.

Harry Beam, a retired Army lieutenant colonel: Hamill, "Design of a Memorial."

126 *Now a potential conspiracy-theorist-in-chief / The NPS asked several:* Fehrman, "Forgotten Memorial.

"Such hate. I'm shocked": Hamill, "Design of a Memorial."

"Any similarities are inadvertent": Rock, "Families of Flight 93."

"We suggested the name be changed": Swauger, "Flight 93 Memorial Challenged."

Congressman Charles Taylor / "For Taylor, a large landowner": Weisman, "Lone Lawmaker."

127 *Citizens Against Government Waste:* Citizens Against Government Waste, "CAGW Names Rep. Charles Taylor."

conveniently used public funds: Fehrman, "Forgotten Memorial."

"Victims' families had to resort to begging": Swauger, "Flight 93 Memorial Deserving."

Instead, he countered with a statement: Reston, "Families Urge Flight 93 Memorial Funds."

His refusal to release the funds: Pace, "Rep. Lifts Block on 9/11 Memorial"; Egan, "Pork No Longer Paves the Road."

128 *Plans for the memorial / After the crash, the Svonavec family:* Last, "Fight over Flight 93."

Armed with the $1 million: Hamill, "Feud over Land Parcel."

The families and the NPS had commissioned / Patrick White, vice president: Last, "Fight over Flight 93."

129 *"It's a very sad day":* Swauger, "Flight 93 Eminent Domain."

Mike Svonavec put up a cash-donation box: Hamill, "Feud over Land Parcel."

"Visitors who want to give money": Worden, "Box of Trouble."

"It's really sad we have to do this": Hamill, "Feud over Land Parcel."

"It is difficult," said Svonavec: Swauger, "'Difficult' Week."

But to Patrick White, the donation box: Worden, "Box of Trouble."

130 *"There were some tears":* Hamill, "Land Dispute Moves Memorial."

He found it in Randall Bell: Collins, "Appraiser of Doom Finds His Niche."

"There was still a lot of debris": "Randall Bell."

Bell proposed / "It's not an emotional issue": Cato, "Owner of Property."

131 *The two-ton, fourteen-foot beam:* Fearon, "Cross Honors Heroes of Flight 93."

132 *Thirty million dollars in private donations:* Bal, "Flight 93 Fundraising Falls Short."

The original plan: Moore, "For Flight 93 Memorial."

A breakthrough came in March: "Families of Flight 93 to Buy 930 Acres."

To end the stalemate: Rock, "Law Change Allows Eminent Domain."

133 *In December 2008, the Flight 93 families:* Hamill, "Land Deal Is
     Reached."
     Even when President Obama assumed office / In May 2009: Courson,
     "Federal Government to Buy Land."
     One of them, Stonycreek Township supervisor: Pickels, "2nd Flight 93
     Memorial Board Member."
     Some of the landowners were surprised: Fiegel and Bouldan, "An
     Emotional Fight."
     On May 3, 2011, Shanksville resident Jeff Ray: "Jeff Ray Speaks."   165

CHAPTER 8

138 *Despite the many emotional ties:* Donna Glessner, personal interview,
     March 2013.
     A returning visitor from Enola: Alex A, TripAdvisor review, April 4,
     2015.
139 *Former President George W. Bush's eyes:* Carpenter et al., "Thousands
     Visit Flight 93 Site."
     "Americans are alive today": "United Flight 93 Memorial Dedication
     Ceremony."
     *Bush was followed / When Vice President Joe Biden / A very different
     take:* Ibid.
140 *Gordy Felt, now the president:* Carpenter et al., "Thousands Visit
     Flight 93 Site."
     "The whole day has pretty much been a challenge": El Nasser, "Flight
     93 Memorial."
     Ilse Homer, whose son, Leroy, was the copilot: Carpenter et al., "Thou-
     sands Visit Flight 93 Site."
     *"Pardon me if I don't look up" / Representative Mark Critz of John-
     stown:* "United Flight 93 Memorial Dedication Ceremony."
141 *One of the last speakers:* Ibid.
     *"Everyone on the flight played a role" / "I don't have a problem with
     honoring":* Lamb, "Flight 93 Families Divided."
142 *When I visited the chapel the following year:* Alphonse Mascherino,
     personal interview, March 2012.
     He had resigned as president: Rock, "Father Al Briefly Steps Down."
     The same year he was diagnosed: Hamill, "Flight 93 Memorial Chap-
     el's New Vision."
143 *Miller's wife, Arlene:* Kalson, "Thrust into the Eye."
144 *Others whose careers changed / For Shaffer, an empathetic listener:*
     Hamill, "Oral Histories Collected."
     "Normally, people have a memorial": Ingold, "The Wife."

145 *Nine years earlier:* Powell, "Shanksville, Pennsylvania."
Sandy Dahl died in her sleep: Ingold, "Sandy Dahl."
By contrast, Dorothy Garcia: Dorothy Garcia, personal interview, January 2014.
Sandra Felt, widow of Edward Felt: Sandra Felt, personal interview, January 2013.
Her brother-in-law, Gordie Felt: Gordie Felt, personal correspondence.

146 *U.S. District Judge Donetta Ambrose:* Lord, "Commission Values Land."
The NPS reported that the memorial: "Flight 93 Memorial Drew Record Number."
Representative comments included: TripAdvisor reviews from shottsinthedarkpara, May 2, 2015; nehasonipatel, April 9, 2015; MissSherlock, September 20, 2014; Rick T, September 24, 2014.

147 *"In my humble opinion":* Cincytraveler44, TripAdvisor review, April 6, 2015.
"A lot of tears were shed there": Chuck Wagner, personal interview, June 2015.
"Memorials, being fixed in concrete and stone": Kimmelman, "Art/Architecture."

148 *"Shanksville's roads are too small":* Asokan, "Shanksville 10 Years Later."
Ernie Stotler, a retired school counselor: Ernie Stotler, personal interview, June 2015.
One frigid day in December: Terry Butler, personal interview, April 2014.

166

Bibliography

The primary source of personal stories in this book is the archive of the hundreds of oral histories compiled via personal interviews by the staff of the National Park Service in Shanksville, Pennsylvania. All oral histories cited in this book are courtesy of the National Park Service, Flight 93 National Memorial, Oral History Project. This material is identified in the notes by the name of the person interviewed and the number of the oral history (for example, Arlene Miller, OH 484).

"'America Is Grateful' to Flight 93 Heroes." *CNN*, September 11, 2002. Online.

Annual Park Ranking Report for Recreation Visitors in 2015. National Park Service. Online.

Asokan, Shyamantha. "Shanksville 10 Years Later: The Same, but Changed." *Washington Post*, September 9, 2011. Online.

Bal, Kecia. "Flight 93 Fundraising Falls Short." *Johnstown Tribune-Democrat*, August 12, 2007. Online.

Berger, Susan. *The Five Ways We Grieve: Finding Your Personal Path to Healing After the Loss of a Loved One*. Boston: Trumpeter, 2011.

Bosak, Pete. "Transcripts Boost Claim that Heroes Intervened on Jet." In *Heroes Were Made*. Johnstown, Pa.: Tribune-Democrat and Johnstown Magazine, 2011.

Brett, Yvonne, ed. *Reflections of Stonycreek, 1776–1976*. Stonycreek Township, 1976.

"CAGW Names Rep. Charles Taylor Porker of the Month." Citizens Against Government Waste, August 21, 2006. Online.

Carpenter, Mackenzie, Sean D. Hamill, Ann Rodgers, and Bill Toland. "Thousands Visit Flight 93 Site for Dedication of Memorial." *Pittsburgh Post-Gazette*, September 11, 2011. Online.

Cato, Jason. "Owner of Property Where Flight 93 Crashed Sues Government over Land Value." *TribLIVE*, October 8, 2013. Online.

Chernus, Ira. "The Meaning of 'Myth' in the American Context." *Mythic America: Essays* (blog). Online.

Chruscicki, Donata, producer. *CBC Nightly News* coverage of (F)Light (video). With reporter Susan Ormiston. 2005. Online.

Clifton, Daniel. "Highland Lakes Dancers Honoring 9/11 Victims." *Daily Tribune*, August 19, 2007, A1, A13.

Clines, Francis X. "Threats and Responses: Flight 93; Pilgrims Flock to Site of Crash Near Rural Hill." *New York Times*, September 9, 2002. Online.

Coile, Zachary, and Henry K. Lee. "Flight 93 Relatives Listen to Tapes." *SF Gate*, April 18, 2002. Online.

Collins, Jeff. "Appraiser of Doom Finds His Niche." *Orange County Register*, April 11, 2013. Online.

Competition briefing book. Flight 93 National Memorial, 2004.

Coomarasamy, Jamie. "9/11 Film Premiere Ignites Debate." *BBC News*, April 25, 2006. Online.

Courson, Paul. "Federal Government to Buy Land for Flight 93 Memorial." *CNN*, August 31, 2009. Online.

"Critics, Proponents Spar over 'Islamic Symbols' in Flight 93 Memorial Design." *Fox News*, September 8, 2010. Online.

Doss, Erika. *Memorial Mania: Public Feeling in America*. Chicago: University of Chicago Press, 2010.

Duryea, Bill. "Keeping Us Rolling." *St. Petersburg Times*, September 8, 2002. Online.

Egan, Timothy. "Pork No Longer Paves the Road to Re-election." *New York Times*, December 25, 2006. Online.

El Nasser, Haya. "Flight 93 Memorial Dedicated to Passengers' 'Valor.'" *USA Today*, September 11, 2011. Online.

Faher, Mike. "Just the Right Person." In *Heroes Were Made*. Johnstown, Pa.: Tribune-Democrat and Johnstown Magazine, 2011.

"Families of Flight 93 to Buy 930 Acres from PBS Coals." Families of Flight 93, March 18, 2008. Online.

Fearon, Peter. "Cross Honors Heroes of Flight 93." *Newser*, August 25, 2008. Online.

Fehrman, Craig. "The Forgotten Memorial: How 9/11 Changed Shanksville, Pennsylvania." *New Republic*, August 24, 2011. Online.

Fiegel, Eric, and Kate Bouldan. "An Emotional Fight over Land for Flight 93 Memorial." *CNN*, May 29, 2009. Online.

First, Josh. "Eminent Domain Only Way to Resolve Flight 93 Memorial Impasse." *PennLive*, May 29, 2009. Online.

"Flight 93 Memorial Drew Record Number in 2012." *NBC10.com*. Online.

"Flight 93 National Memorial Mission Statement." Flight 93 National
    Memorial, National Park Service. Online.
Flight 93 National Memorial newsletter, no. 1. National Park Service,
    September 2003.
Flight 93 National Memorial newsletter, no. 2. National Park Service, May
    2004.
"Flight 93 Never Crashed in the Empty Field Outside Shanksville." U.S.
    Message Board, March 5, 2009. Online.
"Flight 93 Pilot's Wife Recalls Terror of Recording." *ABC News*, April 13,
    2006. Online.
"Flight 93 Public Meeting." In *Flight 93 Advisory Commission Briefing Book*.
    National Park Service, December 9, 2001.
Foote, Kenneth E. *Shadowed Ground: America's Landscapes of Violence and
    Tragedy*. Austin: University of Texas Press, 2003.
Forgey, Benjamin. "Flight 93 Memorial Design Unveiled." *Washington
    Post*, September 8, 2005. Online.
Fraser, Jeff. "Sacred Ground." *H: The Magazine of the Heinz Endowments*,
    Spring 2005, 20–27.
"Frequently Asked Questions—Flight 93 and September 11." Flight 93
    National Memorial, National Park Service. Online.
Freyvogel, Colleen. "Flight 93 Memorial Designs Revealed." *Cumberland
    Times-News*, January 21, 2005, B1–B2.
Garofoli, Joe. "Film Touches Deep Nerve for Families of Flight 93 Vic-
    tims." *SFGate*, April 14, 2006. Online.
Garofoli, Joe, and Chuck Squatriglia. "9/11: Five Years Later." *SFGate*,
    September 11, 2006. Online.
Gibb, Tom. "Flight 93 Crash Site Touted as Memorial to Victims." *Pitts-
    burgh Post-Gazette*, September 20, 2001. Online.
———. "Newsmaker: Coroner's Quiet Unflappability Helps Him Take
    Charge of Somerset Tragedy." *Pittsburgh Post-Gazette*, October 15,
    2001. Online.
———. "Stoic Father Visits Somerset Crash Site of Flight 93 to Say
    Thanks." *Pittsburgh Post-Gazette*, September 20, 2001. Online.
"The Great American Flag Is Unfurled in Western Pennsylvania." Busi-
    ness Wire, September 24, 2001. Online.
Griffith, Randy. "This Is to Remind Us." In *Heroes Were Made*. Johnstown,
    Pa.: Tribune-Democrat and Johnstown Magazine, 2011.
Haddock, Vicki. "Heroes of Flight 93 Honored." *San Francisco Chronicle*,
    September 18, 2001. Online.
Hamill, Sean D. "Design of a Memorial to Flight 93 Fuels Tension Be-
    tween Families." *New York Times*, May 4, 2008. Online.

———. "Feud over Land Parcel Shadows Plans for a Permanent Memorial to United Flight 93." *New York Times*, June 7, 2007. Online.

———. "Flight 93 Memorial Chapel's New Vision at Issue." *Pittsburgh Post-Gazette*, September 9, 2011. Online.

———. "Land Deal Is Reached for a 9/11 Memorial." *New York Times*, January 17, 2009. Online.

———. "Land Dispute Moves Memorial for 9/11 Victims Across a Pennsylvania Road." *New York Times*, July 28, 2008. Online.

———. "Oral Histories Collected from Shanksville Site." *The Blade*, September 11, 2011. Online.

———. "Seven Years Later, 9/11 Hijackers' Remains Are in Limbo." *New York Times*, September 20, 2008. Online.

Hanley, Joanne. *Thoughts on Next Steps*. National Park Service, October 18, 2001.

Hariman, Robert, and John Louis Lucaites. "Vernacular Memorials and Civic Decline." In *The Landscapes of 9/11: A Photographer's Journey*, edited by Jonathan Hyman, Edward Tabor Linenthal, and Christiane J. Gruber. Austin: University of Texas Press, 2013.

Hauser, Christine. "Virginia Tech Sets Out to Preserve Objects of Grief, Love, and Forgiveness." *New York Times*, April 25, 2007.

Hauser, Christine, and Anahad O'Connor. "Virginia Tech Shooting Leaves 33 Dead." *New York Times*, April 16, 2007. Online.

Hawthorne, Christopher. "Reading Symbolism in the Sept. 11 Era." *Los Angeles Times*, October 5, 2005. Online.

Hefling, Kimberly. "N.C. Congressman Blocks Flight 93 Memorial." Associated Press, April 25, 2006. Online.

Ingold, John. "Sandy Dahl, Widow of Flight 93 Hero, Died of Drug, Alcohol Overdose." *Denver Post*, September 14, 2012. Online.

———. "The Wife—Sandy Dahl." *Denver Post*, September 9, 2011. Online.

"International Design Competition." Flight 93 National Memorial, National Park Service. Online.

"Jeff Ray Speaks at the Flight 93 Memorial on May 2" (video). *Daily American*, May 2, 2011. Online.

Kalson, Sally. "Thrust into the Eye of the Flight 93 Storm, She Found Her Calling." *Pittsburgh Post-Gazette*, September 4, 2011. Online.

Kashurba, Glenn J. *Quiet Courage: The Definitive Account of Flight 93 and Its Aftermath*. Somerset, Pa.: SAJ, 2006.

Kimmelman, Michael. "Art/Architecture: Out of Minimalism, Monuments to Memory." *New York Times*, January 13, 2002. Online.

Kraybill, Donald B., Steven M. Nolt, and David L. Weaver-Zercher. *Amish Grace: How Forgiveness Transcended Tragedy*. San Francisco: John Wiley and Sons, 2007.

Kyle, Susan Nicol. "Pennsylvania Firefighter Honors Flight 93 Victims with Flag." *Firehouse*, September 12, 2008. Online.

Lamb, Christina. "Flight 93 Families Divided over Memorial to Passengers' Heroism." *Sunday Times*, September 19, 2010. Online.

Last, Jonathan V. "The Fight over Flight 93." *Weekly Standard*, January 19, 2009. Online.

———. "Precious Medals." *Weekly Standard*, March 31, 2008. Online.

Lester, Patrick. "Chapel Pays Homage to Flight 93 Victims." *Morning Call*, September 5, 2011. Online.

Levin, Steve. "Flight 93 Families Hear Cockpit Tape." *Pittsburgh Post-Gazette*, April 19, 2002. Online.

Levine, Samantha. "Honoring Lives Lost on Flight 93." *U.S. News and World Report*, September 16, 2002. Online.

Lileks, James. "The Sorry State of Modern Civic Memorials." *Newhouse News*, September 14, 2005. Online.

Linenthal, Edward T. "Evil Acts, Sacred Places." In *The Life of Meaning: Reflections on Faith, Doubt, and Repairing the World*, edited by Bob Abernethy and William Bole. New York: Seven Stories Press, 2007.

———. *The Unfinished Bombing: Oklahoma City in American Memory*. Oxford: Oxford University Press, 2003.

Longman, Jere. *Among the Heroes: United Flight 93 and the Passengers and Crew Who Fought Back*. New York: HarperCollins, 2002.

———. "Paul Greengrass's Filming of Flight 93's Story, Trying to Define Heroics." *New York Times*, April 24, 2006. Online.

Lord, Rich. "Commission Values Land Where Flight 93 Crashed on 9/11 at $1.5 million." *Pittsburgh Post-Gazette*, December 9, 2013. Online.

Lovering, Daniel. "Sept. 11 Crash Spared, Transformed Small Pennsylvania Town." Reuters, September 9, 2011. Online.

Lowry, Patricia. "Analysis: Five Finalists' Memorials Try to Capture Impact of Flight 93." *Pittsburgh Post-Gazette*, February 8, 2005. Online.

Lyndon, Donlyn. "The Place of Memory." In *Spatial Recall: Memory in Architecture and Landscape*, edited by Marc Treib. New York: Routledge, 2009.

Mayer, Pamela, and Mike Faher. "Flight 93 Coroner Looking to Future." *Johnstown Tribune-Democrat*, October 20, 2002, C3–C4.

Miles, Donna. "Rumsfeld Pays Respects to Flight 93 Heroes at Pennsylvania Crash Site." American Forces Press Service, March 27, 2006. Online.

Mondello, Bob. "'United 93': Recent Painful History on Film." National Public Radio, April 28, 2006. Online.

Moore, Martha T. "For Flight 93 Memorial, Long-Awaited Progress." *USA Today*, September 11, 2009. Online.

O'Toole, James, Michael A. Fuoco, and Tom Gibb. "First Lady Meets Flight 93 Families at Somerset Site." *Pittsburgh Post-Gazette*, September 18, 2001. Online.

O'Toole, James, and Cindi Lash. "Prayers Memorialize Flight 93 Victims." *Pittsburgh Post-Gazette*, September 15, 2001. Online.

Pace, Gina. "Rep. Lifts Block on 9/11 Memorial." *CBS News*, May 4, 2006. Online.

Perl, Peter. "Hallowed Ground." *Washington Post*, May 12, 2002. Online.

Perry, Steve. "The Marketing of Lisa Beamer." *CounterPunch*, April 1, 2002. Online.

Pickels, Mary. "2nd Flight 93 Memorial Board Member Resigns over 'Eroded Trust.'" *TribLIVE*, May 15, 2009. Online.

Powell, Kimberly. "Shanksville, Pennsylvania—One Year Later." About. com (Pittsburgh), September 12, 2002. Online.

"A Prayer for Our Time" (video). Adastra Design and Video Productions, 2006. Online.

"President Bush Addresses the Nation." *Washington Post*, September 20, 2001. Online.

Quinn, Andrew. "Widow Presses FBI to Release Flight 93 Hijack Cockpit Tape." Reuters, November 27, 2001. Online.

"Randall Bell." Appraisal Buzz, n.d. Online.

Reed Ward, Paula. "Panel Narrows Entries for Flight 93 Memorial." *Pittsburgh Post-Gazette*, January 30, 2005. Online.

Reitman, Valerie. "Afghan Journey Eases a Father's Pain." *Los Angeles Times*, January 22, 2002. Online.

"Response and Recovery: Shanksville, Pennsylvania." Federal Bureau of Investigation. Online.

Reston, Maive. "Families Urge Flight 93 Memorial Funds." *Pittsburgh Post-Gazette*, April 27, 2006. Online.

Rock, Vicki. "The Families of Flight 93: End the Memorial Debate." *Daily American*, May 2, 2008. Online.

———. "Father Al Briefly Steps Down as President of Flight 93 Chapel." *Daily American*, January 19, 2012. Online.

———. "Giuliani Tells Shanksville Students to Believe in Spontaneous Acts of Courage." *Daily American*, June 1, 2002, 1.

———. "Law Change Allows Eminent Domain at Flight 93 Crash Site." *Daily American*, October 15, 2008. Online.

Ruggieri, Eric D. "Reflections on a Day that Changed the World." *American Funeral Director*, September 2002, 26–27, 113–17.

Schrock, Brian. "Down to the Wire: Flight 93 Memorial Designs Make Their Way in Before Deadline." *Daily American*, January 12, 2005, 1.

Schuler, Rhoda. "Pilgrimage to Shanksville, Pennsylvania: Where Heaven and Earth Meet in American Civil Religion." Unpublished paper, 2004.

Setrakian, Lara. "Virginia Tech Students Leave Messages to Victims and Killer." *ABC News*, April 28, 2007. Online.

"Seung-Hui Cho Biography." Biography.com. Online.

Severson, Lucky. "Shanksville One Year Later." *Religion and Ethics News-Weekly*, August 30, 2002. Online.

Shanken, Andrew. "The Memory Industry and Its Discontents: The Death and Life of a Keyword." In *Spatial Recall: Memory in Architecture and Landscape*, edited by Marc Treib. New York: Routledge, 2009.

Shauk, Zain. "Tragedy Victim's Legacy Grows at Lauren's Garden." *Houston Chronicle*, September 10, 2010. Online.

Shermer, Michael. "Why Do People Believe in Conspiracy Theories?" *Scientific American*, December 1, 2014. Online.

Sitler, Helen Collins. "Grieving Ceremonies: Shanksville." In *Western Pennsylvania Reflections: Stories from the Alleghenies to Lake Erie*, edited by Colleen Clemens and Rebecca Beardsall. Charleston: History Press, 2011.

Somashekhar, Sandhya. "Memories of Va. Tech Permeate Gun Debate." *Washington Post*, January 22, 2008. Online.

Stage II Jury Report. Flight 93 National Memorial International Design Competition, September 7, 2005.

Steiner, Frederick. *Design for a Vulnerable Planet*. Austin: University of Texas Press, 2011.

Stone, Benjamin. "Derrill Bodley Killed in Motorcycle Accident." Sacramento City College, September 29, 2005. Online.

Sturken, Marita. *Tangled Memories: The Vietnam War, the AIDs Epidemic, and the Politics of Remembering*. Berkeley: University of California Press, 1997.

———. *Tourists of History: Memory, Kitsch, and Consumerism from Oklahoma City to Ground Zero*. Durham: Duke University Press, 2007.

Swauger, Kirk. "'Difficult' Week for Flight 93 Landowner." *Johnstown Tribune-Democrat*, June 9, 2007. Online.

———. "Flight 93 Eminent Domain Land Grab Unlikely." *Johnstown Tribune-Democrat*, June 7, 2007. Online.

———. "Flight 93 Memorial Challenged." *Johnstown Tribune-Democrat*, September 8, 2005. Online.

———. "The Flight 93 Memorial Deserving of Federal Funds, Too." *Philly.com*, April 30, 2006. Online.

Taussig-Rubbo, Mateo. "Appraising 9/11: Just Compensation Dilemmas from the United Airlines Flight 93 Crash Site." Buffalo Legal Studies Research Paper Series. SUNY Buffalo Law School, January 18, 2013.

Thoren, Laura Emmons. "Flight 93: Memory to Monument." Honors thesis, Dietrich College of Humanities and Social Sciences, Carnegie Mellon University, May 1, 2010.

Tippett, Krista. "Dario Robleto—Sculptor of Memory." *On Being with Krista Tippett*, July 24, 2014. Online.

Toumarkine, Doris. "United 93." *Film Journal International*, April 27, 2006. Online.

Tumarkin, Maria. *Traumascapes*. Melbourne: Melbourne University Press, 2005.

"United Flight 93 Memorial Dedication Ceremony" (video). C-SPAN Video Library, September 10–11, 2011. Online.

"U. Texas's Tower Garden Memorial for 1966 Shooting Victims." Austinist. Online.

Weber, Cynthia. "Popular Visual Language as Global Communication: The Remediation of United Airlines Flight 93." Supplement, *Review of International Studies* 34, no. S1 (2008): S137–S153.

Weeks, Linton. "Heroic Acts to Protect the Word 'Hero.'" National Public Radio, March 9, 2011. Online.

Weisberg, Deborah. "Huge Flag Will Be Unfurled Near United 93 Crash Site." *Pittsburgh Post-Gazette*, September 22, 2001. Online.

Weisman, Jonathan. "Lone Lawmaker Blocks Flight 93 Monument in Pennsylvania." *Washington Post*, April 25, 2006. Online.

We Were Quiet Once. Directed by Laura Beachy. Live Every Breath Productions, 2012.

Worden, Amy. "Box of Trouble at Flight 93 Site: Owner of 9/11 Land Has Kin Angered." *Philly.com*, June 5, 2007. Online.

Wright, Gerard. "On Hallowed Ground." *The Age*, September 9, 2002. Online.

Yates, Jennifer C. "Pa. Locals, Flight 93 Families United by History." *Seattle Times*, November 7, 2009. Online.

Zaslow, Jeffrey. "Near Shanksville, Pa., Local 'Ambassadors' Tend to Flight 93 Site." *Wall Street Journal*, September 12, 2006. Online.

———. "Plans To Honor Sept. 11 'Heroes' Stir Debate over the Definition." *Wall Street Journal*, September 5, 2002. Online.

Index

179

181